Gr...
4321 Trinity Road
Duluth, MN 55811

QUESTIONS ABOUT THE SPIRIT

Here's what reviewers are saying:

"This is the most exciting and outstanding book I have read on the nature and work of the Holy Spirit. . . . Although it is not meant to be a devotional book, I have made it a part of my devotional experience over the past month. This book is too exciting for words. It is an absolute must!"

The Church Advocate

". . . a hard hitting and scholarly work by an evangelical with a past reputation for concise thinking. Chapters are short but plentiful; and it is evident a lot of work went into their production. . . . The book as a whole is important, scriptural, well written, and even brilliant."

...M

"Ramm...   his
thorou...   is
is evid...   it
think...   n
the sp...   y
Spirit,...

"The...   r-
ent; v...   e-
flected...   le
author...   of
the Sp...   n
such...   a-
ture a...   y
grind!...

Great Lakes Gospel Church
4321 Trinity Road
Duluth, MN 55811

QUESTIONS ABOUT THE SPIRIT

BERNARD L. RAMM

WORD BOOKS,
PUBLISHER

WACO, TEXAS

QUESTIONS ABOUT THE SPIRIT

Originally published as RAPPING ABOUT THE SPIRIT, by Bernard L. Ramm

Copyright © 1974 by Word, Incorporated,
Waco, Texas 76703.

First Paperback Printing—February 1977

Printed in the United States of America.
ISBN 0-87680-810-0
Library of Congress catalog card number: 73-85521

Scripture quotations marked RSV are from the Revised
Standard Version of the Bible, copyrighted 1946, 1952,
1956 and © 1971, 1973 by the Division of Christian
Education of the National Council of the Churches of
Christ in the U.S.A. and used by permission.

Scripture quotations marked JB are excerpts from
The Jerusalem Bible, copyright © 1966 by Darton, Longman
& Todd, Ltd. and Doubleday and Company, Inc. Used by
permission of the publisher.

Contents

1. It makes me blush! 7
2. Spirits are hard to get a peek at 11
3. What is hard reality? 17
4. The Spirit is too close to us 22
5. If God is a Spirit, can a Spirit be God? 26
6. The Holy Spirit is a *persona* 32
7. No Son, no Spirit! 37
8. No more spooks! 45
9. God's head start 49
10. Churchly lumber and limbering Spirit 54
11. Rapping about the Spirit 63
12. The Spirit is the only Sapper 75
13. The Hermes from heaven 84
14. Can a bodyless, sexless Spirit love? 94
15. The situation is fluid 99
16. Prof, you have to answer it in this lecture 104
17. Language and/or tongues? 112
18. Charismatics and neo-Pentecostals 119
19. The Spirit and goody-goody Christians 125
20. Does the Spirit have a tongue? 130
21. Prayer as seen from the launch pad 138
22. What has "the one and the many" to do
    with the Spirit? 142
23. Up a tree and don't know it 147
24. The cure for gullibility 152
25. The divine ombudsman 156
26. *In vino veritas* 160

27. A book review won't hurt 165
28. Marcion messes up the Holy Spirit 168
29. The ugly ditch of history 172
30. We close with a poem 175

1.

It makes me blush!

If a person speaks as an art critic, it is presumed that he knows something about art. If he speaks about ethics, it is presumed he has studied ethical theories and has had some reflective moments about his own ethical decisions. The split between ethical practice and ethical theory has been expressed in the popular saying, "Do as I say, not as I do!" Who then should write about the Spirit of God?

Is the presumption correct that it should be a person who knows much about the Spirit in personal experience? But this raises a problem mentioned in Scripture. To profess to know a great deal about the Spirit of God is contrary to the nature of the Spirit of God. There is a hiddenness to the Spirit that cannot be uncovered. There is an immediacy of the Spirit that cannot be shoved into vision. There is an invisibility of the Spirit that cannot be forced into visibility. There is a reticence of the Spirit that cannot be converted into openness. For these reasons one feels helpless, inadequate, and unworthy to write a line about the Spirit.

There is another reason. Should only those who have had great experiences write about the Holy Spirit? Should only those who know experimentally the depths and workings of the Spirit as well as the power of the Spirit be the only ones to write of the Spirit? Although this would seem the case, it is not necessarily so.

I have never spoken in tongues. I have never wittingly healed anybody. I don't know which of the gifts of the Spirit I may have exercised. Like Paul I feel that I am the least of all the saints (1 Tim. 1:13). Nobody has complimented me on my personal

7

piety or holiness or degree of sanctification. Nor am I known as a prayer warrior who gets through when others can't. If man is saved by his good or righteous or religious works, I would be among the first counted out of the running.

For these reasons I blush to write about the Holy Spirit. How can one dare to write about a Spirit who seeks to veil himself, or how can one dare to write on the Spirit when one feels so unqualified experimentally to write on such a great theme?

I blush and yet I write. Paradoxical or mistaken? Perhaps not so. The last person to ask about his great gift as an artist is an artist. It is not the great soloist who teaches music lessons but the music teacher. Nor is the greatest teacher of preaching the accomplished preacher. If such people are asked about the whence and wherefore of their artistic abilities, they will usually give misleading advice.

The reason is that a gift is so much a part of a person that he cannot see it for what it is. That which comes naturally is almost impossible to objectify. When a person is close to his talent, he does not know how his talent functions. It takes the person who stands at a distance from the talent to know how the talent is improved. It is, then, the relatively untalented who teach the talented how better to perform.

So it is with saints. The sainthood of a saint is so much a part of him he doesn't really know how to account for it. If such a person is told he is saintly or Christlike, he is the first to deny it no matter how obvious it is to others. It takes an unsaintly person to see through the structures of sainthood. And so it is in understanding the Spirit.

That which men and women of the Spirit most intently experience is most difficult for them to put accurately into words. True, they write about the experience and seemingly give an objective description of what went on. But this must not deceive us. Like artists and poets, they are the least reliable witnesses of the precise dynamics of their experience. To have a profound experience of the Spirit does not mean that a person can faithfully narrate precisely what happened.

To write on the Spirit, when one feels so distant from the deeper workings of the Spirit, does cause one to blush. But if my analogies above are true, maybe it is the person who is distant from these experiences who can better see their dynamics. Years of studying and teaching Holy Scripture, with its many references to the Spirit, and years of teaching theology, which involves the doctrine of the Spirit, may give an added perspective to the doctrine of the Spirit that those who experience him the most do not have. So as I write on the Spirit I blush and at the same time take courage; what I lack in experience I may compensate for by what I have learned from theological academia.

Bibliographical note:

For an essay on the care with which one should approach the doctrine of the Holy Spirit I commend Abraham Kuyper's *The Work of the Holy Spirit,* vol. 1, chap. 1, sec. 1, "Careful Treatment Required," (Grand Rapids: Wm. B. Eerdmans, 1946). I must confess that I have learned more of the Holy Spirit from Kuyper than any other writer on the subject. *The Work of the Spirit* belongs to every bibliographical note in this book.

This is not a systematic work on the theology of the Holy Spirit. Some of the fairly recent systematic treatments are: George S. Hendry, *The Holy Spirit in Christian Theology,* rev. ed. (London: SCM Press, 1965); Leon Morris, *Spirit of the Living God* (London: Inter-Varsity Press, 1960); Fredrik Wisløff, *I Believe in the Holy Spirit* (Minneapolis: Augsburg Publishing House, 1949); Lindsay Dewar, *The Holy Spirit and Modern Thought* (New York: Harper and Brothers, 1959); Hendrikus Berkhof, *The Doctrine of the Holy Spirit* (Richmond: John Knox Press, 1964).

2.

Spirits are hard to get a peek at

Whatever the great philosophers have said about spirit, the average man to the contrary feels that he is a sense-bound creature. What is real to him is what he touches, hears, tastes, or bumps into. He may be unbearably naïve to the philosopher, but nevertheless his world is the world reported to him by his senses. He moves among objects that are hard or soft, this color or that, one shape or the other, smooth or rough, and light or heavy. He can pound them, beat them, saw them in two, burn them, or pulverize them.

Mr. Average Man also meets people. But people too have qualities. They are thin or fat, short or tall, light-skinned or swarthy, male or female, ugly or beautiful. They have voices that can be heard. They can kick you, shove you, or sweetly kiss you. They take their places among the other objects of Mr. Average Man's world.

The world that surrounds us is also one we sense. We can see rain or sunshine. We can feel hot or cold. At night we can see the moon and the stars. We are familiar with oceans, rivers, lakes, and streams. We know of mountains, deserts, and forests. Here again our environment is one piece with what our senses tell us about objects and about people.

To reinforce it all, Mr. Average Man delights in what this world can offer him. He likes a magnificent car. He saves for years to buy his dream house. He enjoys a delicious meal to the bottom of his stomach! He likes fine clothes and luxurious furniture. A swimming pool, a good game of golf, and a night at the movies are all enjoyed with relish. His pleasures blend into his world of sense, objects, people, things, and the environment.

11

How odd then to introduce the word *spirit* into a conversation. How long is a spirit? Do spirits come fat or thin, pink or green? How do spirits talk and move? How can a spirit which is by definition "immaterial" affect objects which by definition are "material"? How can spirits levitate a table or make a window rattle?

We seem up against a brick wall! As sense-bound creatures spirits seem out of bounds to human beings. We ought to drop the word *spirit* from serious consideration.

But is it that simple? Consider the following experiment. A beam of light is passed through a prism and reflected on a white sheet of paper. We see the typical rainbow spectrum. If we put a thermometer to the right of either end of the spectrum where we see no colors, the temperature of the thermometer rises. That means that there are waves in the electromagnetic spectrum our eyes cannot see. Yet these invisible rays are as real as the visible ones. It would be wrong to say that the only rays that exist are the ones we can see. In fact we know that the human eye sees only a small segment of the electromagnetic spectrum. Some of the most dangerous rays are invisible to the naked eye.

What about our ears? A dog hears a person or a car approaching before we humans do. Evidently he is picking up sound waves that humans cannot. How bats guide themselves has been a mystery for centuries. Now we know that bats emit high-frequency beeps that create echoes which they can hear and enable them to navigate. But the unaided human ear cannot hear these beeps. How premature to claim that the only sound waves that exist are those waves heard by the human ear!

Electricity presents us with another unusual phenomenon. There is no connection between the field of a motor and the armature. Huge diesel-electric locomotives pull freight trains with a hundred cars or more. Yet there is no "power train" as in an automobile. An enormous electrical force is transmitted through space with no connecting rods or gears. This force is invisible to the human eye, yet how powerful!

Gravity is an equally bewildering phenomenon. There have been many theories about how the sun influences the trajectories of the planets. Descartes thought that the universe was filled with minute particles whose swirlings about guided the planets. Later scientists thought of an all-pervasive ether, but no experiment could detect this invisible ocean. We all live in this powerful gravitational field. We know how many millions of pounds of thrust it takes for a space ship to escape the earth's gravitational pull. Yet we cannot feel, taste, nor smell this powerful gravitational field in which we all live.

Then, too, there is that mysterious world of thinking. We conduct our lives by our thoughts. But how long is a thought? Why does one thought seem hours long whereas another flies by in a second, yet both might have the same measurement on a clock? Thoughts have no colors, no shapes, no weights. Yet my whole life is directed by these shapeless, colorless, weightless, intangible thoughts. And the only way I can claim that thoughts may have some tangibility is by an intangible thought!

But the story does not stop here. Sir Arthur Eddington used to talk about two tables: the first table was the table of ordinary perception, and the second was the table of modern physics. The first table was hard, solid, and compact. The second was a fantastic ballet of atomic particles and was more than 99 percent pure space! How much more we have learned of that second table since the days of Eddington! We have learned that there are many kinds of these subatomic particles; that they move at incredible speeds; and that they pack enormous power. The enormous power of atomic bombs is the conversion of a fraction of their masses into pure energy. We are also overcome by the extremely small size of these particles. For example, in one gram of hydrogen there are 300,000,000,000,000,000,000,000 hydrogen molecules. Or to put it in reverse, one hydrogen molecule weighs 0.000,000,000,000,000,000,000,003,3 grams!

What an odd claim it must now be that the only things that exist are what man can grasp directly with his senses! The truth is that the bulk of the materials and events of the universe in which he lives are beyond his powers of immediate perception. Yet the average man goes through the average day in his sense-bound way thinking that what he sees and hears is reality and that reality is what can be seen and heard! To him, this is the real world!

Now let us again introduce the word *spirit*. I am not quite so ready to laugh it off as a primitive superstition. If I am a so-called hard-headed empiricist, I must greatly enlarge my empiricism in view of the state of modern scientific knowledge. If I am a dedicated realist, I must extend what I mean by *reality*.

There are then countless phenomena around us that are hard to get a peek at. Our knowledge of them is indirect. It takes a skilled scientist to detect and interpret most of these phenomena. But they are there and part of reality. A modern hospital will have its department of nuclear medicine, and yet no doctor has seen an atomic particle!

I am not attempting to prove that at bottom the universe is spirit. My point is that I know that there are many realities beyond the ranges of my sense organs, and to confine reality to the immediate report of my sense organs is scientifically an error. Further, most of these realities are hard to get a peek at. It takes special scientific apparatus by the scientist, years of experimentation in laboratory work, and a working knowledge of higher mathematics.

If there is a transsensory world, why may there not be a spirit world? Of course, spirits like electrons are difficult to get a peek at too! If there is such an immense difference between the table of common perception and the table as understood by the physicist, why may there not be a third world—the spirit world? Of course I have something more specific in mind—the reality of the Holy Spirit. If science makes us humble about what our senses miss, why should it not also make us humble about the existence of God's Spirit? If these transsensory realities are so difficult to get a peek at, may not the Holy Spirit be just as difficult to get a peek at?

Nobody is going to turn over a rock and find the Spirit. Nor is he going to inspect his consciousness and find among other objects there the Holy Spirit. No scientist doubts the reality of subatomic particles even though they are so small and so difficult to get a peek at. Why may it not be that there is a Spirit and that he is as powerful as any atomic force and just as difficult to get a peek at? And for all that we would not dare depreciate from his *reality!* So let no scholar, theologian, layman, or scientist think that he is going to encounter the Spirit as he does a door or a dog or a drenching rain! Spirits are hard to get a peek at! Believe me!

"God is a Spirit" (John 4:24). Jesus and the Samaritan woman are discussing the geographical site where God may be experienced and worshiped. Our Lord says there is no such site. Worshiping is a matter of one's inward condition ("in spirit and in truth," John 4:23). The reason is then given that God is spirit. As George Johnston explains, one of the meanings of *spirit* in this passage is *invisibility*.[1] This is the ultimate theological grounds for the difficulty in getting a peek at spirits.

---

1. George Johnston, *The Spirit Paraclete in the Gospel of John* (Cambridge: Cambridge University Press, 1970), pp. 15 ff.

Bibliographical note:

The most thorough discussion of the concept of spirit (and Spirit), with an incredible number of details, is the article entitled *"pneuma,"* by Hermann Kleinknecht et al., in *Theological Dictionary of the New Testament*, 6:332–454. It is a thorough historical study of the concept of spirit from the Greeks to the early church fathers. For a more philosophical and psychological discussion cf. C. G. Jung, "The Phenomenology of Fairy Tales," in *Spirit and Nature*, ed. by J. Campbell (New York: Pantheon Books, 1954), pp. 3–48. For a semipopular discussion of atomic physics in recent research cf. Victor Guillemin, *The Story of Quantum Mechanics* (New York: Charles Scribner's Sons, 1968). Some of the cleverest thinking in refuting a purely mechanical or materialistic understanding of man was done by C. S. Lewis in *God in the Dock* (Grand Rapids: Wm. B. Eerdmans, 1970).

3.

What is hard reality?

"It is by faith that we understand that the world was created by one word from God, so that no apparent cause can account for the things we can see" (Heb. 11:3, JB).

In a crowded reception hall I bumped into a New Leftist who knew that I was an instructor in theology. He came right to the point that was on his mind and asked me what my philosophy was. That question always embarrasses me since I am frightfully eclectic in my philosophical views. I stammered out something to this effect. Then he grinned—but the grin did not deceive me —and asked if I were forced into a corner and had to admit to affinity to one of the traditional schools of philosophy which one would it be. Again being eclectic I don't relish this kind of pushy question, but I said that perhaps it would be some version of idealism which I didn't think was given a fair shake in our century. He replied that he thought as much but that he was dedicated only to that which he could feel, taste, smell, and handle. At that point the crowd jostled us apart so that I could not continue the conversation.

I suspected that behind this New Leftist's questioning he thought anybody with the system or the Establishment would naturally be sympathetic to some version of idealism in philosophy. One could be an idealist and not have to get into the messy social problems of our big cities. Again I am trying to read the vibrations in this short encounter, and I got the "vibes" that the New Left was interested in ghettos, racism, power structures, slums, food, and shelter—all earthy, human, real, tangible sorts of things.

17

As we parted, he again grinned as if I were left with my ethereal, mystical world of idealism where there was no suffering or struggle for justice. Whereas his world was the real, sweaty, hard world that could stink, smell, rot, decay or that could make one feel warm, give one a sense of protection with a substantial roof over one's head, and a feeling of satisfaction from a good meal.

As I left the crowded reception room and walked to my car, I was deep in meditation from this brief encounter. Each step I took meant that my legs had to carry the full weight of my body. The concrete had to stand up under that weight. In order to walk I needed the chemical substance known as oxygen or my muscles wouldn't work. As I got into my car, I thought that I would make it home only by virtue of this intricate piece of fabricated machinery weighing somewhere near two tons. Was all of this hard reality? Is a prison the ultimate example of hard reality because it contains so many tons of steel and concrete?

If the verse which heads this section is true, then all this hard reality of cement, concrete, oxygen, my body, and my car was apparent but not real. It is hard reality, but there is another reality harder than it is! It is a reality harder than steel and more powerful than atomic energy. *That reality is the Word of God.*

This verse does not stand alone in the discussion about what is hard reality. Isaiah wrote: "The Egyptians are men, and not God; and their horses flesh, and not spirit" (Isa. 31:3). Here is typical Hebrew parallelism. The Egyptians are paired with flesh, and God is paired with spirit. And the point of comparison is power! The powerful armies of the Egyptians are powerless before God. The horse, the tank or panzer force of the ancient world, is powerless before spirit. Let us concentrate on the latter for it is more imaginable. A thundering cavalry charge or a mass attack of chariots was the maximum military weapon of that world. Yet Isaiah says that spirit is more powerful than these massive expressions of power via the horse. Spirit is more powerful than horses just as God (a Spirit) is more powerful than armies of men (who are flesh). When it comes to hard reality, spirit is a harder reality than armies or horses!

This is the question I would have liked to ask my New Leftist friend. Is a modern panzer division of military might which he can see and hence sense more powerful than spirit? Or is a modern panzer division nothing before that which he cannot see or sense—spirit?

The writer of Hebrews does not say we sense the Word of God. What we know of the Word of God we know by faith which is another way of saying we know by divine revelation. The same is true of the Isaiah passage. No Israelite ever *sensed* that spirit was more powerful than horses. It is a revelation of God's truth. It is an act of faith to say then that the invisible God is more powerful than a massed army of men, than the powerful array of military might in horses and chariots, and that the visible creations around us are less real and less powerful than spirit!

This statement of Hebrews 11:3 is not a scientific induction. Nor is it a divine revelation of that which man would eventually come to know—that the visible world is composed of invisible specks. Rather it is an affirmation that all the hardness, solidity, and materiality of the universe is based upon something invisible that has more reality, durability, and hardness than the world we see. Thus what my New Leftist friend thought was the final world of substantiality had its substantiality only by virtue of another world. Spirit has more reality than matter; spirit has more hardness than concrete; spirit has more power than atomic energy; spirit has more durability than the so-called constant of energy and matter in the universe; spirit has more concreteness than the car that drove me home from the meeting. But this I know from the divine side through revelation and from the human side through faith. Without divine revelation and without faith I may well suspect the universe of spirit to be wishy-washy and the world that one can smell, taste, feel, punch, pound, smash, and see to be the real world.

Here is the rub! Do my senses refined by science tell me the innermost nature of reality or does divine revelation? Certainly if divine revelation does, it does not detract from whatever science says by its empirical laws. To believe that divine revelation gives us the final clue does not efface whatever clues we have from science. Only an unreflective biblicism would say this.

Nor can we fault men for saying that science tells us what hard reality is when their only source of knowledge is their own powers and what they learn through science. As far as they go, they may well be right. The question is, is there a method that can go beyond science? The biblical answer is that there is. The biblical answer is that the hardest reality is spirit, that the realest of realities is spirit, that the most enduring of realities is spirit, and that the most powerful of realities is spirit. Here then is the modern paradox: that which modern man thinks is the most ethereal and insubstantial of all that he can think of—spirit—is from the Christian standpoint the greatest of all realities. For were it not for the Word of God and the Spirit of God this great universe in its microscopic and macroscopic dimensions would not only have no reality at all, but it would not exist at all. If we want to get to the bedrock of hard reality, we have to get down to the Spirit of God.

Pierre Teilhard was a Roman Catholic Jesuit priest and an expert on the remains of ancient man and paleontology. In theological circles his philosophical theology is one of the more exciting contributions of our generation. On one occasion he wrote, "The felicity that I had sought in iron [i.e., hard reality], I can find now only in Spirit." [1] Teilhard as a rare poet and mystic among the scientists saw through the transitoriness of "iron" to that which was the hard reality of the universe—the Spirit!

---

1. Pierre Teilhard de Chardin, *The Divine Milieu* (New York: Harper & Row, 1960), p. 22.

Bibliographical note:

The modern philosopher who thought spirit a more powerful concept than matter was George Berkeley. So serious were the claims of Berkeley that it might be said that modern philosophy was not possible until Berkeley was refuted. For firsthand acquaintance with Berkeley's thinking see *The Works of George Berkeley*, A. C. Fraser, ed., 4 vols. (Oxford: Clarendon Press, 1901).

4.

The Spirit is too close to us

Theologians have claimed that the New Testament is implicitly a Trinitarian document. It speaks in such an interrelated way of the Father, the Son, and the Spirit. Why did not the Jews of the Old Testament period become binarians? The Old Testament has many references not only to the Lord but to the Spirit of God. Why not a godhead of the Lord and the Spirit?

The usual reason given (and perhaps the right one) is that all references to the Spirit or the Holy Spirit or the Spirit of God are expressions of the immediacy of God's presence and action in his creation. By using spatial metaphors about height, temporal metaphors about time and eternity, and metaphors of power (God's omnipotence) the prophets established the transcendence of God. But using various expressions about the Spirit they taught the immanence of God in creation, in creatures, in natural phenomena, and in man.

When something is brought too close to the eyes, we only see a blur. As we age, we suffer from presbyopia or the inability of the muscles which control the lens of the eye to make necessary adjustments. It is not uncommon to see an elderly person hold a newspaper at arm's length to get the print into focus. So it is with the Spirit.

The Holy Spirit as the immanence of God is so close to us we see only a blur if we see that. The Spirit is so close to us in nature and to our own selves that we can't get him into focus. This is another reason it is so difficult to speak of the Spirit. Yet none of us would be so bold as to say the reality of something depended upon whether we could get it into proper focus!

The closeness of the Spirit as a theological problem can be seen from another direction. It is so very difficult for us to see ourselves as others see us. A person who appears miserly and penny-pinching to his friends thinks that he is acting only prudently about his money affairs. A person who is very hostile in his attitudes toward others assumes that he is playing a safe game with crafty human nature. A person who thinks he has high standards for his office personnel comes across to the personnel as a crab. In each case the person is so close to himself he cannot see himself for what he is. And this is true of virtues as well as vices. This is very similar to the immediacy of the Spirit. He works so closely to us, so very deeply within us, and so mysteriously around us we can never really see him.

The problem is also seen in the philosophy of biology. Some biologists feel that typical mechanistic or chemical explanations of the phenomena of life are not adequate. There seems a mysterious intelligence and force present above the physical and chemical ones. They are prone to call this Spirit. Yet when asked to give a laboratory demonstration of Spirit, they can't do it. If there is a biology of the Spirit, the Spirit is so deeply imbedded into life processes that he cannot be surfaced. One cannot cut open a flower unexpectedly and catch the Spirit unawares. One cannot dissect a creature with such infinitesimal care that he will find a Spirit. Many biological phenomena do point to such a concept as Spirit, but the Spirit is so deeply in the phenomena no laboratory experiment will reveal him. That is the paradox of biology.

This appears to be what John 3 is teaching. Nicodemus can hear the wind howl at night. But in the darkness he cannot see the trees bend or the bushes rustle or the grass bow. He only knows that the wind comes and goes by the sound. So it is with the new birth with the Spirit. No man sees the Spirit come, and no man sees him go! In our language he operates subconsciously, that is, below the level of consciousness. But we do know that we have received the new birth! In giving us the new birth the Spirit is so close to us, so united with the depths of our spirit, that he cannot be seen. But regeneration is no passing religious experience. The Spirit creates us as new creatures in Christ Jesus, and we can bear our witness to this transformation.

Just as the biologist cannot force the Spirit out into the open, neither can the psychologist. Just as no experiment in biology will suddenly reveal the presence of the Spirit, no study or experiment in psychology will show the unequivocal action of the Holy Spirit on the personhood of man. How much we want to force the Spirit into the open! Then, we hope, all would be clear, and we would no longer have to talk religious mumbo jumbo. But the price we would pay would be too dear. The mystery of the Spirit would be simplified; the depth of the Spirit would be made superficial; and the power of the Spirit would be lessened. At the cost of sounding as if we were talking religious mumbo jumbo (and the analytic school of philosophers is sure we are), we must protect the uniqueness of the operation of the Spirit. He is too close to us! Let us not be foolish and try to flush him out into the open as a hunting dog does a covey of birds.

Bibliographical note:

We are indebted again to Abraham Kuyper, *The Work of the Spirit*, bk. 1, chap. 2, sec. 5, "The Principle of Life in the Creature." Some thoughts also come from the historical section of the word *pneuma* in the *Theological Dictionary of the New Testament* referred to previously.

5.

If God is a Spirit, can a Spirit be God?

The New Testament is not written as a book in systematic theology. Theology emerged in the church as various questions were raised and debated. One of these first great questions was: Who was Jesus Christ?

Arius (250–336?) in Alexandria in Egypt affirmed that on his divine side, Jesus was not God as the Father is God but was divine. He could be called a "second god" in that he was the first and great creation of God and through whom all else was created.

Arius was challenged by Athanasius (296–373?) of the same city, who affirmed that Jesus on his divine side was God in the same sense that the Father was God. The controversy grew so intense that the emperor called a council of bishops at the town of Nicaea (near Constantinople, modern Istanbul) in 325. The council decided in favor of Athanasius. Later a second council was called in 381 to polish up the creed of 325. The official Nicaea-Constantinople Creed affirms that Jesus Christ is God in the same sense that the Father is God, hence the meaning of the expression "the deity of Christ."

Athanasius not only had trouble with the Arians but with a group called the Tropici. These theologians had asserted that there was no significant advance of the doctrine of the Holy Spirit in the New Testament from the Old Testament. This bothered Athanasius, but at first he could not see why. Then the light dawned: The problem of the Spirit was no different from the problem of the Son! Is the Spirit a creature like the Son as Arius taught, or is the Spirit truly God as the Council of Nicaea had said of the Son?

Athanasius got his thoughts out into the open and clarified them by writing to a fellow bishop of his, Serapion. In these four letters Athanasius showed that all the fundamental problems about the status of the deity or divinity of Christ applied to the Holy Spirit. Furthermore, that the solution was the same, namely, to affirm that the Holy Spirit was God in the sense that the Son was God and that the Father was God.

A later admirer of Athanasius was Augustine (354–430) who took in hand the problem of the relationship of the Father to the Son to the Spirit. He thus wrote his great work, *On The Trinity*. It is a belabored and repetitious work, but the great theses stand out clearly. There is one true and living God. Christians were not tritheists—believers in three Gods. But within this godhead were three *personae*—the Father, the Son, and the Spirit. Each was equally God and worthy of the same faith, honor, and worship. Thus in Augustine's doctrine of the Trinity the deity of the Holy Spirit is again affirmed.

In a document whose genealogy has been difficult to trace, called the Athanasian Creed because it was believed that Athanasius wrote it, the doctrine of the Trinity was set down in ponderous, repetitious, but terribly clear terms. Its date is somewhere in the fifth century. It spells it out almost mathematically that there is only one God, one Power, one Glory. But there are also three Powers, three Glories, and three Majesties. Yet there are not three gods but one God.

My purpose is not to unravel all the problems of this creed but to show that it is the final step in the full recognition of the deity of the Holy Spirit. From this time on in Christian theology, orthodox theology is Trinitarian theology, and Trinitarian theology is possible only as theologians recognize the deity of the Holy Spirit.

This is first an advancement over the Old Testament. The living God and the Spirit of God are not clearly differentiated in the Old Testament. But now in the light of the New Testament we see the Spirit of God of the Old Testament coming into his full rights as a *persona* of the Trinity.

Second, this is an advancement over any idea of the Spirit as a universal cosmic principle or a universal religious principle. Such a nebulous view of the Spirit and such a generalized conception of his activity is now replaced by the concreteness of the work and *persona* of the Holy Spirit as found in the doctrine of the Trinity.

Third, this means that any retreat from the doctrine of the Trinity such as took place in religious liberalism and in the existentialist theologies of the twentieth century is also a retreat in one's doctrine of the Holy Spirit. All that is gained in richness of understanding the Spirit through the doctrine of the Trinity is lost, and we are back to a vague, nebulous universalized concept of some sort of pervasive Spirit.

We therefore confess that the Father is God, that the Son is God, and that the Spirit is God. In so affirming such a Trinitarian doctrine we affirm the deity of the Holy Spirit. We cannot—and dare not—settle for less.

What could be clearer at this point than 2 Corinthians 3:17–18: "Now the Lord is the Spirit, and where the Spirit of the Lord is, there is freedom. . . . for this comes from the Lord who is Spirit" (RSV). The Lord Christ and the Lord Spirit are so much of each other in their deity that Paul can substitute one for the other!

Appendix: Text of the *Athanasian Creed* (Trinitarian articles).[1]

1. Whosoever will be saved: before all things it is necessary that he hold the Catholic Faith.

2. Which Faith except every one do keep whole and undefiled: without doubt shall perish everlastingly.

3. And the Catholic Faith is this: that we worship one God in Trinity, and Trinity in Unity;

4. Neither confounding the Persons: nor dividing the Substance [Essence].

5. For there is one Person of the Father: another of the Son: and another of the Holy Ghost.

6. But the Godhead of the Father, of the Son, and of the Holy Ghost, is all one: the Glory equal, the Majesty coeternal.

7. Such as the Father is: such is the Son: and such is the Holy Ghost.

8. The Father uncreate [uncreated]: the Son uncreate [uncreated]: and the Holy Ghost uncreate [uncreated].

9. The Father incomprehensible [unlimited]: the Son incomprehensible [unlimited]: and the Holy Ghost incomprehensible [unlimited, or infinite].

10. The Father eternal: the Son eternal: and the Holy Ghost eternal.

11. And yet they are not three eternals but one eternal.

12. As also there are no three uncreated: nor three incomprehensibles [infinites], but one uncreated: and one incomprehensible [infinite].

13. So likewise the Father is Almighty: the Son Almighty: and the Holy Ghost Almighty.

14. And yet there are not three Almighties; but one Almighty.

15. So the Father is God: the Son is God: and the Holy Ghost is God.

16. And yet they are not three Gods: but one God.

17. So likewise the Father is Lord: the Son is Lord: and the Holy Ghost Lord.

18. And yet not three Lords: but one Lord.

19. For like as we are compelled by the Christian verity: to acknowledge every Person by himself to be God and Lord.

---

1. Philip Schaff, *The Creeds of Christendom*, vol. 2 (New York: Harper and Brothers, 1877), pp. 66–68.

20. So we are forbidden by the Catholic Religion: to say, There be [are] three Gods, or three Lords.

21. The Father is made of none: neither created, nor begotten.

22. The Son is of the Father alone: not made, nor created: but begotten.

23. The Holy Ghost is of the Father and of the Son: neither made, nor created, nor begotten: but proceeding.

24. So there is one Father, not three Fathers: one Son, not three Sons: one Holy Ghost, not three Holy Ghosts.

25. And in this Trinity none is afore, or after another: none is greater, or less than another [there is nothing before or after: nothing greater or less].

26. But the whole three Persons are coeternal, and coequal.

27. So that in all things, as afore said: the Unity in Trinity, and the Trinity in unity, is to be worshiped.

28. He therefore that will be saved must [let him] thus think of the Trinity.

This rather lengthy treatment may be compared with the Creed of Nicaea (381) which is an improvement over the statement of 325 but not adequate enough for the Holy Spirit: "And [I believe] in the Holy Ghost, the Lord and Giver of Life; who proceedeth from the Father; who with the Father and the Son together is worshiped and glorified; who spake by the prophets. . . ."

Bibliographical note:

The article on "spirit" (*pneuma*) in the *Theological Dictionary of the New Testament,* 6:332–454, reveals how the Jews wavered between a concept of the Spirit as a synonym for the power and presence of God and to think of the Spirit in personal, individualistic terms, finally succumbing to the former. The important materials on Athanasius are contained in C. R. B. Shapland, ed., *The Letters of St. Athanasius Concerning the Holy Spirit* (London: Epworth Press, 1951). Cf. Augustine, *On the Trinity* (for which many editions and translations exist, but cf. Edinburgh: T. and T. Clark, 1878). John Calvin has a significant, but not always appreciated, essay on the Holy Spirit and Trinity: *Institutes of the Christian Religion,* I/13 (we suggest the latest translation in the *Library of Christian Classics,* vols. 20, 21). Barth's treatment of the Trinity is ranked with Augustine's and Calvin's: *Church Dogmatics,* I/1, chap. 2 (Edinburgh: T. and T. Clark, 1936). Showing that references to Trinitarian materials in the New Testament are not sparse but abundant is Arthur Wainright, *The Trinity in the New Testament* (London: SPC Press, 1962).

6.

The Holy Spirit is a *persona*

All talk about the Trinity gets us tongue-tied! The Latin word *persona* meant first the mask of the actor, then the role of the actor, then the character of the actor. This was the word used in forming the doctrine of the Trinity. However, our modern word *person* means an individual, so "three persons" leads to a doctrine of tritheism.

Another Latin word used was *modus* or mode. This too was suggested. However, it seemed that God incarnate appearing in history as Jesus of Nazareth was more than a *modus* of the divine Being—the Son.

The New Testament seems to teach more than monarchism. Monarchism teaches emphatically that God is one (as in Judaism and Islam) so as to eliminate any possibility of Trinitarianism. Although the New Testament speaks of the Father, Son, and Holy Spirit, it never does so in denial of the unity of God: God is one Lord, not three. How does one correlate the emphasis in harmony with the Old Testament that God is one with the frequent association in the New Testament of the Father, Son, and Spirit?

Christian theologians have taught through the centuries that the doctrine of the Trinity is a mystery. That is why the theologian who really understands his doctrine of the Trinity does not seek to illustrate it by analogies in creation or man. I agree heartily with Mühlen in his great book on the personality of the Holy Spirit when he wrote that "the mystery of the Holy Trinity is the central mystery of Christianity." [1] This means that the doctrine of the

1. Heribert Mühlen, *Der Heilige Geist als Person* (Münster: Verlag Aschendorff, 1966), p. 1, s. 1.02.

Trinity can never be completely rationalized, that is, explained with no remainder. There is always a remainder. Every time we say one we must say three, and every time we say three we must say one. The word *persona* is of much material help in enabling us to state the doctrine of the Trinity as clearly as we can.

It is not my purpose to go into the doctrine of the Trinity with the thoroughness of Mühlen but to exploit what is contained in the word *persona* for the doctrine of the Holy Spirit. At minimum it means that in some sense the Holy Spirit is personal.

Our problems immediately begin! There is no Hebrew or Greek word that is a one-to-one correspondent to our word *person*. Karl Barth has reminded the cult of personality of our day that the entire Holy Scripture was written without the word *person* (see bibliographical note). But the Holy Scripture does speak of God in a very personal way. The word is lacking but not the idea. The Scriptures nowhere teach that God is impersonal or beyond the personal.

If the Spirit is at least personal, then we may no longer think of him as only an influence, only a power, only a cosmic principle, only a synonym for the divine presence and/or power of God. When religious liberalism broke with the doctrine of the Trinity, it had to retreat from the riches of the doctrine of the Spirit as contained in the doctrine of the Trinity. This is ever so clear in *The Spirit*, edited by B. H. Streeter (1921). In contending for the personhood of the Holy Spirit we are also contending for the rich set of personal relationships believers may sustain with the Holy Spirit.

All the relevant verses on the personhood of the Spirit are reviewed in substantial books on systematic theology. I need not rehearse these verses. However, I want to make three points: (1) It is easier to think of the Father and Son as persons because we know persons who are fathers and sons. We do not know any person who is a spirit. It takes some mental effort to think of a spirit as a person and even more the Holy Spirit. (2) Mühlen shows how the expression *we* in John frequently includes the Holy Spirit. *We* is a term about persons, so to speak of we and include the Spirit is to imply that the Spirit is a person. (3) The word *spirit* is grammatically a neuter, and we usually don't attribute personality to an it. For this reason it is easier to think of the Spirit as a principle rather than as a person. On the other hand, who takes sexuality seriously in grammar? *La plume* is the French for pen and is feminine, whereas *le crayon* is the word for pencil and is masculine. There is certainly no sexual difference between the two. Therefore we must cut loose from grammar and see that a word that is grammatically neutral is actually used for a person.

Once a Christian thoroughly grasps the personhood of the Holy Spirit his understanding of the Spirit should be transformed. He now sees that all his relationships with the Holy Spirit are with a person. Each one of the many relationships of the believer to the Spirit as set out in the New Testament is now understood as a personal relationship. The believer or the church that does not enter into the riches of this discovery is the poorer for it.

There is another basic sense in which the personhood of the Holy Spirit is to be understood by the Christian. If we use the expression "that is the person of the king," we mean more than that the king is a person. We mean that there is royalty and a dignity that goes with being a king. Similarly to speak of the Holy Spirit as a person is more than to say that he acts personally. It implies the dignity, majesty, holiness, and exaltedness of the Spirit.

One of the ancient Christian heresies about the Son is that of subordinationism. This means that in some sense Jesus is not fully God or fully deity. He is of a lower order than the Father. We can also have the subordinationism of the Spirit. We do this when we relegate the Spirit in our worship and in our conception of him to a being less than deity. The Creed of Athanasius certainly protected itself from any notion of the subordination of the Spirit. However, in typical Protestant piety that is not fully informed of the historic doctrine of the Trinity, there does exist the subordinationism of the Spirit. Somehow we do not accord to him the full rights of deity. But when we duly recognize the personhood of the Spirit in the Trinity, we recognize all the royal rights and dignities which pertain to a member of the Trinity.

There are many things attributed to the Spirit in his relationship with Christians. We cannot detail out all these relationships, for that is a book in itself. The point is that when we are being related to the Spirit we are being related to a person. As a person he is our counselor. As a person he is our instructor in truth.

As a person he helps us in our prayers. As a person he aids in the victory of spirit over flesh. As a person he makes our bodies temples of the living God. How greatly would our Christian experience be enhanced if we truly understood that all the Holy Spirit does for us and in us and with us is done by the Spirit who is a person.

Bibliographical note:

The concept of person is usually discussed with reference to the doctrine of the Trinity. Cf. Karl Barth, *Church Dogmatics*, I/1, pp. 400ff. However, I have not come across any work in English as thorough as that of Heribert Mühlen, *Der Heilige Geist als Person*, 3rd ed. (Münster: Verlag Aschendorff, 1966).

The Greek word *hypostasis* is used for "person." However, in the New Testament it has the more customary philosophical meaning of "reality." Its meaning of person is a later philosophical and theological development. For an extensive treatment of the word, cf. Helmut Köster, *"hypostasis,"* in *Theological Dictionary of the New Testament*, 8:572–589.

7.

No Son, no Spirit!

The heresy of Arianism asserted that Jesus Christ with respect to his divine nature was not very God of very God, but like God (*homoi-ousia*). He was God's first and highest creation through whom he created all other things. The Council of Nicaea decided in favor of saying that Jesus on his divine side was of the identical (*homo-ousia*) essence of the Father and therefore very God of very God or true God of true God.

In spite of this decision at Nicaea, Arianism did not disappear. One of the places it again manifested itself was in Spain in the sixth century. In order to add one more nail to the Nicene Creed and thoroughly repudiate Arianism, another word was added to the Nicene Creed (Third Council of Toledo, A.D. 589). It was the Latin word *filioque*, "and the Son." The Holy Spirit proceeded not only from the Father as Nicaea said, but he also proceeded from the Son. If the Spirit can proceed only from God, then to say that he proceeded from the Son means that the Son is God as much as the Father is God.

Adding *filioque* to the Nicene Creed and having this addition accepted in the West greatly agitated the Eastern Orthodox church. It was one of the major reasons for the separation of the Eastern church from the Roman Church in A.D. 1054. It is not my intention to adjudicate this controversy, but the *filioque* did say something which the New Testament clearly teaches: there can be no pneumatology without a foregoing Christology. That is why one of the titles of the Spirit in the New Testament is "the Spirit of Christ." In more common language, we must never break away our doctrine of the Spirit from our doctrine of Christ. Or, the Spirit must never be separated from Christ.

The entire plan of redemption and revelation in Scripture is Trinitarian. The Father, Son, and Spirit are one in all that they do, and what each does complements the other. If one cannot separate the Son from the Father, neither can one separate the Spirit from the Son. But as a matter of fact we do. These kinds of separation where the Spirit in principle is broken off from the Son I strongly protest.

Mysticism is one manner in which the Spirit may be broken away from the Son. In the sense that the mystical is parallel to the hidden, Christianity cannot divorce itself from mysticism. Our "mystical union with Christ" means that our union with Christ is hidden. Whenever we pray, we believe that we are in immediate, mystical contact with the Father. There is no danger in this kind of mysticism.

There is a tradition of a more articulate mysticism in Christianity in both the Roman Catholic and Protestant communions. These mystics frequently refer to themselves as "Christomystics," or they believe in a "Christomysticism" (for example, Deissmann, Schweitzer, Stewart). However, in Christomysticism there are two gravitational fields. The first is Christ, and the second is mysticism as such. As long as a Christomystic keeps Christ-centered, danger is averted. But if the Christomystic becomes enamored with mysticism as such, he soon finds himself more mystic than Christian. He wants to include all mystics within his mysticism. When he does that, he breaks the Spirit away from Christ, for he has an experience induced by the Spirit but not centered in Jesus Christ. This temptation to drift from Christomysticism into mysticism per se is very great, and I protest it as it violates what the *filioque* is trying to say: One cannot have a pneumatology without a Christology!

Another temptation to separate Christ and the Spirit is to be found in *enthusiasm*. Enthusiasm is used in a special way in theology. It means an extreme emphasis on the psychological or experiential elements in religious experience. In some instances it borders on fanaticism. In all cases there is a great emphasis placed on the emotional stirrings in religious experience. Although it is usually thought of as an eighteenth-century movement, it should not be so limited. Existentialism of today may be an alternate version of enthusiasm.

The reason enthusiasm was so disdained in the eighteenth century is that that century was the century of reason. Men whose concept of Christianity was very rational considered emphasis on the emotions to be downgrading the intellectual dignity and sobriety of the Christian faith. The most famous encounter of those times was between Bishop Butler and John Wesley. One of the most rationalistic defenses of the Christian faith was Butler's *The Analogy of Religion* (1736). On the other hand, Wesley was the man of the burning heart and the man to whom the witness of the Spirit was a deeply emotional and moving experience. When Wesley came into Butler's territory, Butler ordered him out because he considered the kind of religious experience Wesley attempted to generate as a very horrid thing.

In a wider perspective enthusiasm represents any appeal to heightened emotions or unusual experiences. Parallel to this is the enthusiast's conviction that what he experiences is inspired by the Holy Spirit. He may jump, roll, talk in tongues, see visions, or have unusual inward feelings such as "waves and waves of divine love."

Today most theologians would accuse the age of reason of underplaying the role of emotion, imagination, and trust in religious experience. The enthusiasts were not all wrong. Furthermore theologians do attribute vital Christian experience to the Holy Spirit. There can be no debate at this point.

However, the temptation of the enthusiast is that of the mystic, namely, the experience becomes an end in itself. When this happens, we can say in theological language that the Spirit has been broken away from Christ. The New Testament emphasis is always first on the person and work of Christ and second on man's experience of grace. It is really exceptional how little the New Testament does speak of the psychological, emotional, and experiential aspect of salvation. When enthusiasts of whatever school reverse this New Testament emphasis, then in part or in whole they have separated Christ and the Spirit.

Let us come at this from another angle. It is the ministry of the Spirit to point men to Christ, to lead men to Christ, to illuminate man's mind about Christ, and to glorify Christ in the believer. The danger of the enthusiast is that he makes the most central work of the Spirit the psychological or emotional effects in him. Hence, what is of maximum importance is what he experienced, or what he felt, or what special manifestation of the Spirit he enjoyed. The emphasis of the work of the Spirit is thereby transferred from Christ to the experience of the enthusiast. And to do this is to separate the Spirit from Christ.

Another manner in which the Spirit may be broken away from Christ is by intensive, psychological introspection. This may take many forms too. Victorious life movements or overcoming movements or higher life movements or deeper life movements may cause the Christian to engage in perpetual self-inspection to see if he has "it." Since God wills our sanctification, there is a summons to every Christian to live a life beyond the ordinary. With the best of intentions Christian people will systematize sanctification into some kind of method or scheme. Then the problem of the Christian is whether he is conforming to the scheme. This can only be done by endlessly inspecting one's interior psychological state. Such states are supposedly induced by the Spirit. When the Christian gets caught up into this scheme of sanctification or victorious life and gives a vastly disproportionate amount of his time and spiritual energies to self-inspection, he is breaking the Spirit away from Christ. One's own internal state has become more important than the objective criterion of conformity to the image of Christ.

As psychiatry and clinical psychology have progressed in their knowledge of the workings of the self, their findings have been picked up within the church and put to spiritual service. The Christian well-versed in psychological dynamics can be caught in the same trap as the victorious life Christian. Granted he is perhaps a far more sophisticated and knowledgeable person, but the same temptation is there. Questions of self-identity, self-acceptance, understanding one's sexuality, and relating to other people are of paramount importance for Christians. The temptation in this instance is to turn one's entire Christian life into a kind of psychological adventure. One's psychological life becomes the focal point of one's entire Christian life. We are caught betwixt and between. Too many orthodox, evangelical, and conservative groups are very ignorant of man's psychological processes and suffer much from this lack of knowledge. On the other hand, those initiated into personal dynamics are tempted to make it the whole game of Christianity. Both fall off the log although at different ends. However, my concern is with those who fall off the log at the psychological end.

There can be no question that every spiritual experience is also a psychological experience. Nor is there any question that every Christian is also a person with a certain psychological make-up. Further, much harm has been done to Christians in churches, schools, and mission societies because administrators have not understood these distinctions. But it is also a fact (to which I can bear witness for I have seen some tragic developments from it) that Christians can be so caught up with the psychological aspect of human experience that the objective, Christ-given elements have dropped out of sight.

My contention is that when this happens the Spirit is broken from Christ. I mean by this expression that whatever experiences a Christian has, and whatever psychological dynamics he may live with, the goal and measure of the Christian life is Christ. When Christ becomes secondary to psychological considerations, then the Spirit is broken away from Christ, and this is heresy.

The next example of breaking the Spirit away from Christ is a touchy and difficult one. This is the issue with Pentecostalism. On the one hand the Pentecostal churches certainly hold to the great affirmations about the person of Christ and the gospel which is centered in Christ. No one can fault them at this point.

But then what are we to think of the following statement:

> The Assemblies of God exist expressly to give continuing emphasis to this reason-for-being [raison d' etre] in the New Testament apostolic pattern by teaching and encouraging believers to be baptized in the Holy Ghost.[1]

In addition to this, groups that have Pentecostal in their name or in their doctrine make the Pentecostal experience of paramount importance. The question is: Have they broken the Spirit away from Christ? Is it not odd that the Christian church should be identified in terms of the Spirit rather than of Christ? Do the

1. General Council of the Assemblies of God, *Statement of Fundamental Truths* (Springfield, Mo.: Gospel Publishing House, n.d.).

theologians among the Pentecostal groups truly understand the issue involved in the word *filioque?*

When Pentecostalists preach the gospel, there is no question that they keep the Spirit and Christ together. But the serious question is: Does not the enormous emphasis Pentecostalism (in all its branches whether bearing the name or not) places upon the Spirit, the Baptism of the Spirit, and speaking in tongues as a manifestation of the baptism of the Spirit actually split the Spirit off from Christ? Or to put it another way: Do Pentecostal theologians really understand the depths of the *filioque* question? Or yet again, has Pentecostalism really come to theological maturity in the way it relates its Christology to its pneumatology? Or pressing even harder, does not the identification of a denomination in terms of the Spirit rather than in terms of God or Christ as a matter of fact represent a breaking off of the Spirit from Christ?

To the degree that the Spirit takes precedence over Christ in Pentecostalism's practice and theology, Pentecostalists break the Spirit away from Christ; to the degree that they are Christocentric in preaching and theology, they avoid the danger.

I shall discuss the current charismatic movement or so-called Neo-Pentecostalism later, but I mention it at this point for the specific content of our discussion. The charismatic movement is confessedly a movement about the Spirit of God. It therefore faces the traditional temptations of all movements that center so much attention on the Spirit of God and Christian experience. Does it escape the danger of separating the Spirit from Christ? Certainly any movement which does as a matter of practice separate the Spirit from Christ cannot have claim to authentic Christian experience. Again I can only ask the question: Does the new charismatic movement make so much of the Spirit and so much of the subjective, internal experience that it in principle separates Christ and the Spirit? This is a searching question which must not be lightly dismissed.

Peter set down the criterion for Christian growth: "Instead, go on growing in the grace and in the knowledge of our Lord and savior Jesus Christ. To him be glory, in time and in eternity. Amen" (2 Pet. 3:18, JB). Any growth in the Spirit or any going into the depths of the Spirit must meet this criterion. Otherwise the Spirit and Christ are divided.

If what has been said in previous paragraphs is true, one is most filled with the Spirit when one is most conscious of Christ and least conscious of the Holy Spirit. The Holy Spirit glorifies Christ, not himself. This is the humiliation of the Spirit which parallels the humiliation of Christ in his incarnation. If we are ever sure that our Christian experience is Christ-centered, we preserve the intention of the *filioque* and recognize that the Holy Spirit is truly the Spirit of Christ.

Bibliographical note:

That Pentecostals are in the main-line orthodox tradition for their basic theology see Nils Bloch-Hoell, *The Pentecostal Movement* (London: Allen and Unwin, 1964), pp. 95ff. For the necessity of a Pneumatology built on a Christology see G. W. Bromiley, "The Spirit of Christ," in *Essays in Christology for Karl Barth* (London: Lutterworth Press, 1956). For Calvin's classic attack upon those who separate the Spirit and Scripture, hence by implication Christ and Scripture, see *Institutes of the Christian Religion*, I/9. For the dangers inherent in mysticism see B. B. Warfield, "Mysticism and Christianity" (*Biblical and Theological Studies*. Philadelphia: The Presbyterian and Reformed Publishing Company, 1952), pp. 445–462. For a defense of Christomysticism see James S. Stewart, *A Man in Christ* (London: Hodder and Stoughton, 1935). For a critique of the new group therapy, etc., see Thomas C. Oden, *The Intensive Group Experience: The New Pietism* (Philadelphia: Westminster Press, 1972).

Bound to be a classic for some time to come in Pentecostalism is Walter J. Hollenweger, *The Pentecostals* (London: SCM Press, 1972). Very revelatory of the very immature theological character of the Pentecostal movement is its inability to really understand the doctrine of the Trinity and the doctrine of justification by faith. How can any theology be a healthy, biblical theology if it cannot get two such great doctrines into focus? And if it cannot, how easy it is to violate the meaning of the *filioque* and break the Spirit away from Christ.

8.

No more spooks!

Albert Outler wrote: "This understanding [of the Holy Spirit] is the death knell of superstition." [1]

If the Spirit is in, the spooks are out! The range of spookery is very great. It is difficult to know where it stops. The most obvious case of spookery is animism. Animism is the religion of primitive peoples who believe their immediate world is surrounded by good and evil spirits. Religion, if not most of life itself, is seeking means to ward off the evil or bad spirits and wooing the favor of the good spirits. According to Holy Scripture there is only one all-powerful, all-good, divine Spirit, and that is the Holy Spirit! As soon as a person understands the biblical doctrine of the Holy Spirit, then he is done with the spookery of animism.

Beyond the range of animism itself as the religion of primitives are a series of practices followed by men who may or may not be animists. This is but another version of spookery. Holy Scripture is strong in its denunciation of such practices as trying to contact the dead, or bring their spirits back, or to practice magic, and so on (Exod. 22:18, Deut. 18:9–11, Ezek. 13:17–23, Acts 8:9–24, Acts 16:16–18, Gal. 5:20, 2 Tim. 3:13). The penalty of such practices was death (Exod. 22:18, Lev. 19:26, 31, 20:6, 27).

In all of these practices is the presumption that some spirit or spirits are at work in things, for rituals in themselves are powerless. Once a person grasps the biblical doctrine of the Holy Spirit

---

1. Albert Outler, "Veni, Creator Spiritus: The Doctrine of the Holy Spirit," *New Theology No. 4*, ed. Dean Peerman and Martin Marty (New York: Macmillan, 1965), p. 198.

all such practices become meaningless as well as blasphemous. Furthermore, there is a blessed deliverance, for when the Spirit is in, the spooks are out!

The prevalence of astrology in Western society is unbelievable. Tons of its literature are on typical drug store and supermarket reading racks. There are even special sections—a phenomenon no other type of literature enjoys. Most of our large daily papers contain a horoscope. Believers in astrology do not believe that they are superstitious or that they are dealing with spooks. Certainly there is a difference between popular astrology where a person feels he has his own mystique about himself geared in with the sign he was born under and that mystique guides him through life, and the very intricate schema of a professional who has a very detailed knowledge of astronomy and the complicated rules for the interpretation of different heavenly configurations.

However, astrology, too, ventures into forbidden territory. The ban against all methods to circumvent God's immediate lordship in his world and among mankind applies to astrology. Granted a professional astrologer is far more sophisticated than a primitive animist and his crude magic; nonetheless, they are both in the same camp. Furthermore, in all the talk I have heard from people addicted to astrology and chattering about being Libra or Pisces or Leo, I have never yet heard one speak of how their astrological concern spilled over into the moral character of their lives, or how they learned to love better, or the great compassion they received for the suffering of the world. It may be there, but it doesn't come out in their conversation which uniformly is highly introverted, subjective, and if I may play judge, selfish.

Spookery is a form of idolatry. Idolatry means any kind of belief, religious or nonreligious, which assigns man's destiny to anything within this cosmos in ignoration of the living God whom one psychologist of religion defined as the Determiner of Destiny. Most peoples in civilized countries have some traces of superstition left in them. Even those who deny it most vigorously will admit to some if prodded hard enough about all of their beliefs. Superstition is wicked because it assigns good and evil to man solely by virtue of the power of the superstitious object— the amulet or the superstitious ritual. The Christian conviction is that if the Spirit is in, the spooks are out, and the Christian who best understands his doctrine of the Holy Spirit is freest from spookery.

Consider how superstitious we are about the number thirteen! And the "we" are the "we" of the atomic age, the space age, the technological age, the age of the explosion of college education, the age of the universal library of the paperback! How many skyscrapers have a thirteenth floor? How many motels, hotels, and hospitals have a room thirteen (including such numbers as two hundred and thirteen)? Note the numbering in an elevator where mysteriously the usual serial order of numbers is interrupted as it skips from twelve to fourteen! How apprehensive we all are about the terrible portent of Friday the thirteenth. One has to ask: is there more fear in American people over the number thirteen than there is of the living God? "It is a fearful thing to fall into the hands of the living God" (Heb. 10:31).

There are many other forms of spookery in our American life. It is the Christian conviction that whenever a person turns his life over to spookery—astrology, tarot cards, tea leaves, palm reading, handwriting analysis, and so on—and lets some aspect of spookery control his weal and woe, then he has gone completely contrary to Holy Scripture. The Holy Spirit and spookery are 100 percent incompatible. Once a person grasps the greatness, majesty, and power of the Holy Spirit and his work in creation and providence, then the spooks must go. What a wonderful experience to be under the control and guidance of the Spirit of God rather than the bewildering world of spookery.

Bibliographical note:

For an analysis of astrology among the young as a case of a mis-placed faith in God see John C. Cooper, *Religion in the Age of Aquarius* (Philadelphia: Westminster, 1971). In the long history of astrology there have been different kinds of astrology. We refer here to *judicial astrology*, in which it is believed that the sign of the zodiac under which one is born (i.e., the sign in ascendancy at the hour of one's conception or birth) and the "house" (general astronomical con-figuration) help forge the character and destiny of the person.

9.

God's head start

One of the many meanings of *head* is "to advance in front of.'
Hence a head start means to get the advantage over somebody
in a foot race. It is also used in a situation where a slower running
person is given an advantage by letting him start sooner or letting
him start from a position ahead of the others. In recent American
political life it referred to a special program for children handi-
capped by racial discrimination, poverty, and all the debilitating
effects of a depressed or slum neighborhood. I am using the term
in this latter sense, for all sinners are deprived, depressed, and
spiritually debilitated persons. The only cure for such backward
children is a divine head start—a new birth by the Holy Spirit.

Of course, the sinner does not feel or know that he cannot please
God without a divine head start. He thinks that if he keeps the
Ten Commandments or the Sermon on the Mount or is sincere
in his moral intentions he is acceptable to God. The average man
is usually guilty of the "Kantian error." Immanuel Kant (1724–
1804) is generally considered the greatest modern philosopher
(modern meaning from Descartes to the present). Kant reduced
religion to ethics or morality. His work *Religion With-in the
Limits of Reason Alone* (1793) affirms that religion as a set of
dogmatic beliefs and supernatural events for our salvation is out;
only a religion compatible to reason is permissible, and that is a
religion which restricts itself to ethics.

Whenever a person thinks that he pleases God by his good
works or moral character or ethical seriousness or good intentions,
he is guilty of the "Kantian error."

The "Kantian error" is illustrated in Nicodemus. Nicodemus

was a religious man. More than that, he was an outstanding religious man—a leader in Israel, a Pharisee! If a man is acceptable to God because he is sincere, moral, and religious, Nicodemus had it made. But when Jesus told Nicodemus that he must be born again (John 3:7), Jesus meant that Nicodemus was not acceptable to God with all his sincerity, morality, and religion. He needed a divine head start! We shall never become Christians until we free ourselves from the "Kantian error."

In the New Testament the "Kantian error" was the mistake of the Galatian churches. They presumed that by faith in Christ *and* keeping the Mosaic law they would be saved. To them the gospel was grace plus morality, Christ and Moses, the cross and good works. Paul said this was an impossible combination. To believe in it was to be an apostate from grace (Gal. 5:4). No one can be saved or acceptable to God if he is an apostate from grace. To believe the "Kantian error" is to be an apostate from grace. Only the new birth by the Spirit, God's head start for deprived sinners, can undo the "Kantian error."

Jesus said to Nicodemus that he *must* be born again. There is a special word for "must" in Greek—*dei*. It is a little self-contained verb. It is one of John's favorites, used of both the crucifixion of Christ and the resurrection, indicating a divine necessity or a divine imperative. No man can get around the new birth! The kingdom is open only to those who have been born anew.

Why this *must?* Why must we have a divine head start by the Holy Spirit? Jesus gives the answer: We are flesh! (John 3:6). Flesh is humanity in its weakness. It cannot do the will of God (Rom. 8:7). Flesh is also hostility to the truth of God. The man in flesh is at enmity with God. Flesh is also man in his sinfulness. Sinners cannot enter the kingdom. Only by the new birth from above (or again or anew) can there be divine power for human weakness, divine peace and reconciliation for man's enmity, and God's cleansing (Spirit and water, John 3:5). Flesh also means to be Spirit-less!

If man *must* be born again, and can *only* be born again by the Spirit of God, what can a man do about his own new birth? In the words of Nicodemus, "How can this be?" (John 3:9). The answer is John 3:16. God's love has provided an atonement for sin—that is derived from the meaning of verse 15 (the lifting up of the serpent by Moses) and the meaning of *gave* in verse 16. This atonement has been made by God's only son. This *son* must be understood in all the richness of the father-son relationships spelled out in the entire Gospel of John. His son died on the cross. Now if somebody believes in this son and this death on the cross (in the analogy of the serpent lifted up in the wilderness), then that person will have eternal life—will be born again!

This is the head start all men need. All men are flesh, and all men are sinners. No man can save himself by any moral or religious program or even self-sacrifice. There is no *autosoterism* —salvation by one's own efforts—in Scripture! There is only the divine head start in the new birth by the Spirit of God.

Historically, what did a new birth or being born again mean in the world of Nicodemus? How did the rabbis use the term? Fortunately the scholars have dug this out for us. To be born again meant the following to the Jews at that time:

1. It meant to be converted to a certain religion as the truth of God. Proselytes who became Jews were considered born again. Hence, for Nicodemus to be born again meant not only faith in Christ as the crucified Messiah (John 3:15) but also acceptance of the whole Christian faith.

2. It meant to experience an act of creation in the same manner in which God created the world. A born-again person was a newly created person. So faith in Christ is a spiritual new creation.

3. It meant that the past life of the proselyte ceased to exist. His new life in Judaism was such as to wipe out his past existence. In a similar but not identical vein Paul says that when a person is a new creation in Christ all the things of his old life have passed away. This is a very vigorous picture of repentance! There is no new birth without repentance.

4. The Jews considered all of God's action as a begetting. So to be born again by God means to be subject of a divine action within one's soul or heart. This emphasizes that man is flesh and cannot save himself; to the contrary being born again is such an important act that only God can perform it.

5. Being personally born again is an anticipation when all things shall be born again—*palingenesis! Palingenesis* was the Jewish term for the restoration of all things (Matt. 19:28, used in Titus 3:5 for personal regeneration). Hence the experience is eschatological; it anticipates the glorious future and the future glory.

Bibliographical note:

For comments on the text of John 3 I recommend the excellent and full discussion by Leon Morris: *The Gospel According to John* (Grand Rapids: Eerdmans, 1971). For the meaning among the rabbis of being born again, cf. Friedrich Büchsel and Karl Rengstorf, *"gennaō,"* etc., in *Theological Dictionary of the New Testament*, 1:665–674. For a most comprehensive article on "flesh" (Greek, *sarks*) with special attention to John's Gospel, cf. Eduard Schweitzer et al. in *Theological Dictionary of the New Testament*, 7:98–150.

10.

Churchly lumber and limbering Spiri

From the human, visible aspect, the church is a society or an organization which in many ways functions not too differently from many other societies in our communities. From the divine side it is the body of Christ and the temple of the Holy Spirit. From the human side it is governed by officers, but from the divine side it is governed by the risen Lord through his Holy Spirit present within the local church. This is a nice theory, but it can falter miserably in practice. Some have put the dilemma in these terms: To what extent is the church an organism drawing its vitality and unity from the Holy Spirit, and to what extent is it an organization made up of much churchly lumber?

We can't have it either/or. From the purely human standpoint, any group of men must have a minimum of organization if it is to be effective in the smallest degree. From the standpoint of the New Testament, officers in the church are specified (bishops, deacons, teachers, and so on). So to be true to the New Testament we must have some of the organization it authoritatively instructs us to have. At the same time the church is more than another human organization. Being the body of Christ, it has its unity and life in the Spirit. Furthermore, those men who are officers are expected to be men filled with the Spirit. If such officers are not men of the Spirit, then the church degenerates into a pile of churchly lumber.

But which comes first in the order of our priorities? How do we balance the life of the church so that the Spirit can properly work through organizations and that organizations are kept limber for the ministry of the Spirit?

The classic historic study of this problem is that of Hans von Campenhausen, *Ecclesiastical Authority and Spiritual Power*.[1] In barest essence his thesis is that Christ and his apostles were primarily charismatic (men of the Spirit) persons and their authority was recognized in view of their spiritual power. However, as the church expanded geographically, grew in size numerically, and had to face ever new problems, the officers in the church tended to be less men of the Spirit and more men of ecclesiastical authority. The end of the line is Cyprian, died A.D. 258 (for von Campenhausen limits his study to the first three Christian centuries), bishop of Carthage, to whom the organization of bishops is the church. The bishop is a man of ecclesiastical power not of charismatic, spiritual leadership (although in fairness to the Roman Catholic system it must be said that it presumed the Spirit was present in the entire Roman Catholic church and in a special way in its priests, deacons, and bishops).

This development is true to one of the generalized observations of sociologists. Movements start with much spirit, enthusiasm, and sense of unity. They have great psychological momentum going for them. As time proceeds and more officers are needed, more rules become necessary, the ideals of the founders of the movement grow dim, and suppressed problems appear, the movement loses its original charismatic character and becomes more and more a bureaucracy. Rules have become more important than ideals; procedures have become more important than persons; and keeping the status quo has become more important than being creative and innovative. What started as limber spirit has ended up as organizational lumber.

This observation is frightening! How can the church avoid this degeneration from the vitality of the Spirit into a lumber yard of churchly organization? If it finds itself more lumber than Spirit, how does it recover its original Spirit-generated charismatic quality? What sharpens the dilemma is our previous observation that a church of pure Spirit is impossible. A minimum of organization in the church is necessary however small it may be. Yet these little toothpicks of organization can eventually become a lumber pile which buries the Spirit beneath it.

---

1. Stanford: Stanford University Press, 1969.

Furthermore, the New Testament sets down no formula about the relationship of how much Spirit to how much lumber. We can appeal to no chapter or verse as our compass in this problem. The best we can do is to suggest something programmatic: The church must always be aware that it is to be first a church of the Spirit, then of organization; that it should be aware of this fatal process of degeneration from a spiritual organism into a churchly lumber yard; and, that it must think of how it can periodically renew itself.

The classical example of the church slipping from its nature as a temple of the Holy Spirit charismatically endowed by the Holy Spirit into an impersonal, cruel ecclesiastical machine is to be found in Dostoevsky's story of the Grand Inquisitor.[2]

Ivan, who tells the story, calls it a poem, "an absurd thing but I would like to tell you about it." The story takes place in Seville, Spain, in the sixteenth century at the height of the Inquisition. The Grand Inquisitor, the cardinal of the city, is tall, severe, and ninety years old. On one particular day he had burned to death one hundred heretics for the glory of God. The next day Jesus appears in Seville. He has been lonely for his children and wants to walk with them once more as he had in ancient Palestine. The Christians are people of the Spirit. They do not need someone to point out Jesus and say, "There he is!" (I am doing some improvising!) Nor does Jesus need to say, "Here I am! Recognize me!" The people know spontaneously that it is Jesus and flock to him and follow him everywhere. Jesus then begins to heal people as he did during his earthly life. He comes to the steps of the cathedral just as a funeral procession emerges, bearing the corpse in a white casket of a seven-year-old child. Will he raise the dead as he did in ancient Palestine? This is the thought that floods into the minds of the people. Yes, he will! He stops the procession. The mother of the dead child throws herself at his feet and cries out, "If it is thou . . . then raise my child from the dead!"

The coffin is lowered to the ground. Jesus gazes into it and says what he once said in ancient Palestine, "Talitha cum." The little girl sits up with eyes wide open, a smile is on her lips, and

2. Feodor Dostoevsky, *The Brothers Karamazov*, vol. 1, part 2, bk. 5, sec. 5 (Middlesex: Penguin Books, 1958).

she gazes around. There are cries and sobs among the people.

Just at that moment the old cardinal, the Grand Inquisitor, is passing by wearing an ordinary monk's garb and not his royal cardinal's attire which he wore the day the hundred heretics were burned to death. He immediately demands the arrest of Jesus. The people who are so used to obeying his commands put up no resistance and let the soldiers arrest Jesus. The Grand Inquisitor blesses the people and passes on.

Jesus is put in a "dark, narrow, vaulted prison in the old building of the Sacred Court" and is locked up by the soldiers.

The Grand Inquisitor awaits his time and then at night comes to him and says, "It is you. You." Then the Grand Inquisitor gives a long speech. The main burden of it is that Jesus came promising men freedom, but freedom is a terrible responsibility. Accordingly the Roman Catholic church made a bargain with men. If men will surrender their freedom to the church, the church will give them happiness. This has been a bargain sealed and settled for centuries. Jesus has no right to return to earth and jeopardize this bargain. Men would sooner enjoy happiness than bear the terrible burden of freedom, so why should Jesus return and condemn men to terrible freedom?

During this lengthy speech Jesus says nothing. The Grand Inquisitor is vexed and wants Jesus to say something "however bitter and terrible." To the contrary Jesus suddenly rises, comes to the old man of ninety years, and "kissed him gently on his bloodless, aged cheeks. That was all his answer." The old man is so taken aback that he opens the door and tells Jesus to leave and says, "Go, come no more—don't come at all—never, never." The prisoner goes through the door and away.

Then comes the terrible indictment: "The kiss glows in his heart, but the old man sticks to his idea."

This is one of the great masterpieces in literature, and I have sketched just the part which serves our purpose. I have been discussing the dilemma of the church that while it must be a charismatic church because it is the church of the Holy Spirit, at the same time it must be a church with a minimum of organization. The story of the Grand Inquisitor is the church become demonically organization and completely bankrupt charismatically. The cardinal rules from the sheer authority of his office and not one shred from the command of his spirituality. It is a church that is so fanatically organizational that it would sooner have its own game to play with Jesus absent rather than enjoy the wonders of the presence of the living Lord. In fact, in the legend it is said that the cardinal would sooner have Jesus imprisoned and tortured than have him freely walk the streets of Seville bringing untold blessedness to its citizens.

Look at the irony of it! What can warm the heart of a ninety-year-old man? The kiss of Jesus! Yet the cardinal would sooner play his game of churchianity than enjoy the wonders of that kiss!

The power of the legend of the Grand Inquisitor is that it is an extreme case. But the legend has repeated itself endlessly in the history of the church. It is said that Dostoevsky had a special hatred for the Roman Catholic church, but this does not change one whit the real intention of the legend of the Grand Inquisitor. The Grand Inquisitor walks the land whenever people in ecclesiastical position prefer their authority to the spirituality of the church. The Grand Inquisitor is there whenever denominations consider their programs or their literature or their resolutions beyond challenge and use every means possible to silence the person or persons who want the voice of the Spirit to be heard again in the land. The Grand Inquisitor lives again whenever churches prefer their programs to the presence of the living Lord.

Whenever a pastor becomes pure churchman, pure peddler of programs, or pure pusher of schemes, he comes close to the spirit of the Grand Inquisitor. Playing church is more important than the living Christ. The organization is more important than the Spirit. This is one reason the organization man in the Christian denomination is usually upset by the new charismatic movement. Efficient organizations are predictable; charismatics are not. "Proper channels" give the organization man a sense of security; the spontaneity of the Spirit gives him anxiety. Success can be easily measured by increased budgets, increased size of the congregation, and increased programs. How does one put a charismatic experience down on the ledger of church success?

Denominational organizations can also come close to playing the role of the Grand Inquisitor. Here is where the lumber is usually piled the highest and defended most vigorously. But this is also a most effective way of stifling the Holy Spirit. The Grand Inquisitor and the Holy Spirit are eternal enemies! The Grand Inquisitor did not live and die in Seville in the sixteenth century. He appears again and again in the history of the church.

Dostoevsky has shown us the demonic situation which can exist in any church or denomination when organization becomes an idol and destroys the organism of the Spirit in the church. First, it is a stupid mistake because it buries the Spirit beneath ecclesiastical lumber. But more than that, it is demonic because it chooses to play the irrational game of churchianity no matter the spiritual cost to the church.

The theologian of recent times who has made the most of the distinction of the church as a highly organized institution as over against the church as a vital instrument of the Spirit is Emil Brunner.[3]

In developing his ideas Brunner uses the German word for church (*Kirche*) to stand for the church as ecclesiastical lumber, and the Greek word for church (*Ekklesia*) to stand for the church as primarily a temple of the Spirit. Brunner considers it tragic that the church has almost exclusively become a *Kirche* and not an *Ekklesia*. Part of the inspiration of this doctrine of the church came from Rudolph Sohm and the other from the state-church concept which yet prevails in Switzerland. According to Brunner the *Ekklesia* is a Spirit-filled, Spirit-guided community. Such concepts as community, fellowship, and charismatic are central to his idea of the *Ekklesia*. Of course he knows that there can be no *Ekklesia* without some of the organization of the *Kirche* and that the *Kirche* may still retain vital elements of the Spirit derived from the church as *Ekklesia*.

However, the same pulsebeat is to be found in Brunner as in Dostoevsky. Brunner is afraid of the mentality of the Grand Inquisitor which puts so much a premium on organization, structures, formalities, and power. He wants to restore the *Ekklesia* to the Spirit-filled church of the Book of Acts where the emphasis is on the spiritual life of the church and its believers and not upon the *Kirche* as an established Spiritless organization.

---

3. *The Christian Doctrine of the Church, Faith, and the Consummation, Dogmatics,* vol. 3 (Philadelphia: Westminster, 1962).

How can a church live in the dilemma as a pilgrim church which at the same time must be a church of the Spirit and a church of the officers? The first step in learning how to live with this built-in problem is to recognize it. That sounds trite but it is not so trite. If there is always the Grand Inquisitor coming back again and again to make the church purely ecclesiastical power, there is the enthusiast or fanatic who wishes to completely rob the church of all its organization in order to make it a free church of the Spirit. We can't have it one way; we can only have it both ways. Denominational leaders must realize they can become Grand Inquisitors and that the church without the Spirit is nothing more than a human religious society. The church can never escape this uneasy compromise between *Kirche* and *Ekklesia.*

The second step is to recognize the matter of priorities. The church as the abode of the Spirit is prior to the church as the organized community of God's people. Both are abstractions as I have pointed out several times already. But since both must co-exist, they can only co-exist as God would have them to co-exist if they straighten out their priorities. The church of the Spirit has the priority over the church as the organization. One can have a true church of Christ with much Spirit and little organization; one cannot have a true church of Christ that is all organization and no Spirit.

Third, one of the mottos that came out of the Reformation was "the church always reforming" (*ecclesia semper reformanda*). The Reformers knew that they no more could attain perfection in the church than the Roman Catholics could. One could not think therefore of "one big bang Reformation" that would set the church on the straight course and in internal purity once for all. Pure doctrine and holy living must be a continuous effort, and so the church must be continuously reforming.

Continuous renewal is no easy thing! Traditions always harden. Men in places of power become puppet Grand Inquisitors. That which is wayward in life, practice, and doctrine takes on the aura of the normal when practiced long enough. Sometimes those who seek renewal are short on patience and understanding. It is easy to confuse butchery with surgery. All of this means that there is no plan of renewal that is failproof. But we must do our best to keep the church a church of the living Spirit and not of ecclesiastical lumber!

The continuous study of Scripture is one such procedure. This must not be purely academic interpretation or pious observations drawn from different biblical texts. It means studying Scripture in such a way that God may confront the church and the individual in the Word. Intense personal and corporate prayer is another such means. How hard it is to pray without preaching! Or to pray keeping God at arm's distance! Or to pray without going down the deep rut of clichés! Yet out of prayer can come insight and strength. Confession of sin has become a lost art, but in Scripture it is one of the foundations of the spiritual life. The danger of corporate confession—which well may be proper—is that it gets us "off the hook" as far as our own moral integrity is concerned.

We Protestants who have said so many harsh things about the Roman Catholic church should now be very contrite. Nothing in Protestantism in our century has come anywhere near the renewal (*aggiornamento*, "bringing things up to date") which John XXIII started in the Roman Catholic church culminating in the famous documents of Vatican II. The Roman Catholic church is deliberately and consciously attempting to unload so much of its ecclesiastical lumber collected through the centuries in order that once again it might be what it claims to be—the body of Christ enlivened by the Holy Spirit! Are we Protestants so divided and so deviant from the original biblical revelation that *aggiornamento* is an impossibility for us? We hope not! We hope that in the wings there is an Origen, an Augustine, a Thomas, a Luther, a Calvin, or a Wesley who can cause the winds of the Spirit to blow powerfully through the church once again!

Bibliographical note:

Abraham Kuyper struggles with this problem in his chapter 39 entitled "The Government of the Church" in *The Work of the Spirit*. Søren Kierkegaard's fiery attack upon the Spiritless church of Denmark will be found in his work *Attack upon "Christendom"* (Princeton: Princeton University Press, 1946). Some of the irony and sarcasm is priceless. Barth, like Brunner, is also restless with the church-state arrangement in Switzerland which violates the nature of the relationship of the Spirit to the church. See his attack in section 62 of the *Church Dogmatics*, IV/1, entitled, "The Holy Spirit and the Gathering of the Church." Seeing a new inbreathing of the Spirit in the church, J. Rodman Williams has written *The Era of the Spirit*, in which he not only discusses the renewal of the Spirit but the beliefs of leading theologians about the Spirit (Plainfield: Logos International, 1971).

11.

Rapping about the Spirit

Rapping is one of the words of the younger generation. It replaces the older bull session and buzz group as an expression. It stresses more spontaneity and adventure with conversation. It reduces the no-nos to a minimum as far as possible avenues of exploration are concerned. So let's do some rapping about the Holy Spirit.

We want to "bust open" the doctrine of the Spirit. By "busting open" we mean to rap on a lot of subjects concerning the Spirit that are usually left unmentioned or insufficiently treated. By rapping we shall endeavor to enrich our concept of the Spirit. We need richer imagery of the Spirit than that of pure power or presence.

1. *The Holy Spirit and beauty.* Have you ever connected the concept of the Spirit with the production of beauty? After being redeemed from Egypt and given the law, the Israelites were instructed through Moses to build a beautiful, movable tent of worship (Exod. 25–40). It is usually called the tabernacle after the Latin word for tent, *tabernaculum.* If Egyptian art of the ancient kingdoms is a clue to its beauty, it was really beautiful!

However, to create a tent of beauty takes artists. Where was Moses to get artists in the semiarid land of the wilderness of sin? Most of the Israelites had spent their years as slaves building the storehouses of the pharaohs. The narrative tells us that Hur and his assistants were to be filled with the Spirit of God so that they could make the artistic objects and designs in gold, silver, stone, and "for every craft" (see Exod. 31:1–6, 28:3, 35:30, 36:1–2, 38:22–23).

63

God has been called the Great Mathematician, the Great Engineer, the Great Architect, and the Great Designer. Has he ever been called the Great Artist? The closest to this is in Dorothy Sayers's book, *The Mind of the Maker*.[1] Miss Sayers says that God in creation worked like an artist but since she is not an artist she must work in a territory with which she is more familiar. That is the creative work of a novelist, and Miss Sayers has written a number of mystery stories and a play (*The Man Born to be King*, 1943). Accordingly she draws many parallels between the creative working of a novelist and God's creative activity. In the texts from Exodus cited above, the production of beautiful objects and beautiful decorations is made possible by the enablement of the Holy Spirit!

As I have already proposed, the work of the Spirit is direct. The Spirit sustains an immediacy with the creation, the creature, and man. If any member of the Godhead is to move the fingers of man so that he may create an object of beauty, it must be that ever-present, always-immanent Holy Spirit. So our first "busting open" of the doctrine of the Spirit is to enrich our understanding of the Spirit by seeing that he is a Spirit who creates beauty.

It is true that Scripture does not make too great an emphasis on art and beauty. There is a general reticence in Scripture about plastic and representational art. Behind this is perhaps the fear that works of art which represent spiritual reality may usurp the place of that reality. Overemphasis on the plastic beauty may be a version of idolatry.

Of course, this can also be underestimated. Throughout Scripture, God is a God of glory, and glory is beauty made manifest. The God of Scripture is a beautiful God! Unfortunately, very few theologians have ever stopped to discuss this aspect of God. The God whom Sartre rejects could never be the God of Scripture, for he is a God of beauty, and therefore there is nothing ugly or repulsive in him that any man should wish to reject him.

Back to the Holy Spirit. The Spirit of God is a producer of the beautiful. He can put into man's fingers and hands those talents which in turn will produce objects of beauty. This means there is something of beauty in the Spirit. Here is where the enrichment begins! Ordinarily we think of the Spirit in terms of power

1. New York: Living Age Book [1917].

and immanence. That is a rather barren Spirit. But if we add to our understanding of the Spirit that he has a dimension of beauty in his nature, then we automatically enrich our understanding of the Spirit. We do not imply that a philosophy of aesthetics (of beauty and the beautiful) can be extracted from our understanding of the Holy Spirit. As great a temptation as that might be, there are not enough biblical materials to allow us to do that. But on the other hand, it reminds us that we cannot separate beauty from the Spirit!

2. *The Holy Spirit and creation.* The first mention of the Spirit in Scripture is in Genesis 1:2. Some commentators believe that "wind" is a better translation than "spirit," for they are identical words in the Hebrew as with *pneuma* in the Greek. John 3 contains a play on both meanings of the word. There is a reason for sticking with the older translation of Spirit in Genesis 1:2.

The Holy Spirit is associated with creation in other texts of Scripture (see Ps. 10:29–30, Job 33:4, Isa. 40:13). The presumption of the text seems to be that the Spirit not only broods over the primeval chaos but that he is the energizing presence of God in the other six days. God speaks his word, and the word becomes realized because the Spirit is present in the cosmos in order that the word be realized. This is congruent with our earlier assertions that the Spirit is the immediate, immanent, direct, and powerful touch of the Godhead upon the cosmos and man.

Creation is more than the exertion of power! Production of machinery is more than the use of power machines. Behind each product is a blueprint. The Holy Spirit is not only the power of God in his cosmos, but as the wisdom of God he is the blueprint of creation. In traditional terms the Holy Spirit is the Spirit of teleology or design.

Modern science is caught between a rock and a hard place. If we take the human body as representative of all creatures, we find it a collection of highly engineered organs and complex, interrelated chemical systems. The human eye, composed of organic materials and occupying less than one cubic inch of space, is a marvel in light perception, color perception, depth perception, and motion perception. The ear is also highly engineered. The external ear cups the sound and sends it into the first membrane. There it is mechanically transmitted by three tiny bones intricately balanced and connected to each other. These bones vibrate the second membrane which in turn vibrates a fluid. The fluid vibrates the hairs sticking up into it. As the hairs bend, they stimulate the nerves at their roots, which stimulates the auditory nerve which sends the impulse to the brain.

The body has mechanical marvels such as the arch of the foot, which absorbs stresses so that we are not jarred, and the backbone, which can be held erect or can be flexed.

Modern science knows all of this and mountains more. Yet modern scientists oppose any teleological (design) explanation of these phenomena or any designer. Final causes (the central concept in teleological explanations) were judged by Bacon (1561–1626) to be virgins, and modern scientists agree. Just as virgins give birth to no children, so final causes are not fruitful concepts for scientists. Surrounded by mountains of teleological materials modern scientists plod their unteleological way.

But there is always a small minority who insist on rocking the boat of science. Driesch thought the only way life could be understood was to presume that it was governed by directives ("entelechies"). Morgan talked of creative jumps with unpredicted emergents in the ongoing of evolution. Bergson taught that evolution could be understood only if one presumed an *élan vital* which shoved life on and gave it direction. Jeans and Eddington believed that some version of philosophical idealism was the logical outcome of modern science. Whitehead saw science pointing toward a panpsychism and a panentheism (that is, matter is at bottom spiritual and the cosmos is permeated by the active presence of God). Errol Harris has written a learned treatise in science and philosophy maintaining the thesis that the universe is understood fully only in its creative and holistic aspects and not through dissection and analysis.[2]

There is no doubt about these matters in Scripture. The Spirit of God is the member of the Trinity who touches the creature. Whatever the creature has, he has by virtue of the Holy Spirit. This theological assertion is independent of the theory of evolu-

2. *The Foundations of Metaphysics in Science* (London: George Allen & Unwin; New York: Humanities Press, 1965).

tion whether it is true or false. Whether the process is immediate or slow, a groping or a direct act, the Spirit is the divine teleologer.

We cannot push beyond that. We cannot create a biology of the Spirit which solves all the problems of biology. One may affirm that from the perspective of divine revelation the Spirit is the *élan vital* in nature and yet not be able to convert the insight into a workable philosophy of biology.

Our concern is not to solve problems in science but to enrich our understanding of the Holy Spirit. The Spirit must be seen as more than sheer power or pure immanence. If he is a Spirit of beauty, he is also a Spirit of wisdom as seen in his relationship to creation.

3. *The Holy Spirit and healing.* According to the Gospel narratives the Holy Spirit is the great healer. Already in the Old Testament the God of Israel is a God who heals (Num. 12:13, Deut. 32:39, Exod. 15:26, Ps. 103:3). One of the reasons suggested to explain why the Hebrews did not make advances in medicine like the ancient Egyptians and Greeks is that they attributed healing to Yahweh and therefore did not feel the necessity of developing their own human healers. When Christ returned from his temptation, he began his public ministry filled with the Spirit through whom he healed many people. The importance of the association of the Spirit with the healing ministry of Jesus is that the unforgivable sin or blasphemy against the Holy Spirit arose out of his healing ministry. The Spirit is the finger of God, which means the concentrated, focused power of God. Peter says in a sermon in the book of Acts that Jesus went around doing good by the power of the Spirit (Acts 10:38).

If our theses to this point are valid, it comes then as no surprise that the Holy Spirit is the healer. There can be healing only when there is the immediate touch of God on the creature, and it is the Holy Spirit who provides that touch.

Man's ills, pains, and death are the consequences of his sin. Healing is not merely a physical process. Healing is always set in a redemptive context. Even where this might not be obvious, as in instances in the New Testament, it was still the case. The healing of the body is one of the ways in which God's love and redemption reach out effectively and efficaciously to man. It is within this theological presupposition that the Spirit heals.

As a divine healer the Holy Spirit is then also a Spirit of redemption. Each member of the Trinity participates in his "thing," and the "thing" of the Holy Spirit is to make redemption a reality in human experience in a number of different ways. One of those things in redemption is healing, and so the Holy Spirit is also the healing Spirit.

4. *The Holy Spirit and holiness.* The Spirit is called a Holy Spirit because he is a person with a compassion to create holiness in persons. Both the Father and the Son are holy. However, as each *persona* of the Trinity has his thing, it is the unique ministry of the Spirit to be occupied with holiness.

One of the great vacancies in ethical theories from the Greeks to the present is that they do not contain any doctrine of the Holy Spirit. Part of the uniqueness of biblical ethics is that the doctrine of the Holy Spirit is at the center of its ethical system. The Holy Spirit is the motivator in Christian ethics. An ethical theory without a realistic doctrine of motivation is but a paper theory. Such great chapters as Romans 8 and Galatians 5 reveal that the power in Christian ethics is the presence in the spirit or heart (both terms are used) of the Spirit of God.

Holy Scripture recognizes that the determination of the right must be correlated with the power to will the right. That is why the greatest tract on sanctification in Scripture—Romans 6–8—is more occupied with the power to do the right than with the determination of the right. It is an empty ethical theory which believes it can determine the right or good but offers no theory how men concretely achieve the right.

How do we motivate sinful men? What power will boost a man out of his selfishness and greediness? The philosopher Kant had some feel for this problem. He taught on purely philosophical grounds that man would need the equivalent of the new birth mentioned in the Gospel of John. Unfortunately, Kant's philosophy had no Holy Spirit who alone can give the new birth.

The presence of the Holy Spirit in the moral life of the Christian is also suggested in Ephesians 4:30. Paul says that by sinning the Christian grieves the Holy Spirit. Among other things this reveals the passionate concern of the Holy Spirit for personal holiness in Christians. There is no legalism here where Spirit interacts with spirit. It is not wrath which is evoked but suffering.

Christians have endlessly been accused of being either legalists or Puritans. If they have been, they have the New Testament out of focus. Where men are guided, energized, and led by the Holy Spirit, as the New Testament teaches, there is no place for legalism or whatever is bad about Puritanism. Essential Christian morality is not imposed as a code or legal prescript, but it is written on the human heart—the wellspring of action—by the Holy Spirit. So says Hebrews 10:15–16.

That the Holy Spirit is the author of personal holiness in Christians is also taught in James 5:5. Granted it is a difficult verse, it does seem to say that the divine Spirit is in contest with the human spirit as it seeks to sin. The result is that the Christian is paralyzed to act—a motif similar to Romans 7. The point is that the Holy Spirit is in the heart of the Christian exercising his moral presence. In the positive sense he is creating personal holiness.

5. *The Holy Spirit and the human spirit.* One of the complaints of recent writers on the theology of the Holy Spirit is that not enough has been said historically of the relationship of the Spirit of God to the spirit of man. I shall attempt to interact with that concept now as I see it.

The Holy Spirit is not only the promoter of sanctification in the Christian, but he is also the promoter of man's spiritual life—a phrase I like better than man's religious life. This is taught clearest in Psalm 51. The historical background was apparently David's adulterous affair with Bathsheba, his indirect murder of Uriah, and the stunning rebuke of Nathan ("thou art the man"). In this psalm of penitence in verses 10–11 (JB) David writes:

> God, create a clean heart in me,
> put into me a new and constant spirit,
> do not banish me from your presence,
> do not deprive me of your Holy Spirit.

David's fear is that his sinning has cost him his spiritual life. His heart threatens to be insensitive to God and his worship. David needs to be assured that the possibility of a spiritual life is restored. From the human side he needs a clean heart and a new and constant spirit. From the divine side he needs the Holy Spirit. Hence he prays, "Do not deprive me of your Holy Spirit." If the

Holy Spirit no longer functions in David's heart, a spiritual life is no longer possible.

Taking our cue from this psalm, we then affirm that one of the significant operations of the Spirit is to help foster a spiritual life in the believer. Without the help of the Spirit, we would not want to sing the songs of Zion or wish to hear them sung. Without the Spirit, prayer would become a burden and eventually an impossibility. Without the Spirit, the Word of God is not honey in our mouth (". . . sweeter also than honey and drippings of the honeycomb," Ps. 19:10, RSV). How could the psalmist have composed such a lengthy and tremendous psalm to the Word of God unless he had an appetite for that Word energized by the Spirit (Ps. 119)? How can a man truly love as God loves and truly wish for the salvation of man as God does unless the divine Spirit is working along with the human spirit? Fewer things are more painful to the man of God than to enter one of the dark nights of the soul when spiritual things seem so impossible to enjoy and experience with relish.

It is the Holy Spirit who makes possible religion *in me*. Religion *pro me* is that which God does for me and external to me such as giving divine revelation, sending his Son for the world's redemption, and sending his Spirit on the day of Pentecost. Religion *in me* is how I personally appropriate and experience what God has done *pro me*. Faith, trust, obedience, worship, and service are all my ways of responding to that which God has done for me. Because this territory is so much the locus of the action of the Spirit, one of the expressions of a really spiritual man is that he is filled with the Spirit (Eph. 5:18–20). Hence, to be filled with the Spirit is to be in a state where the Holy Spirit is fully activating man's spirit in man's spiritual life.

Spirituality is the hidden commerce between God's Spirit and the human spirit. Spirituality is possible only because God's Spirit indwells the Christian. Granted, men may be religious without being spiritual because all men possess to some degree the divine image—the *imago dei*. Being religious and being spiritual we think are two different things although both stem from the possibilities in the divine image. Furthermore, like all commerce between God and man there is no conceivable way of marking out the boundary line which differentiates what man's spirit does and what God's Spirit does.

Basic to understanding this relationship is what Paul wrote in Philippians 2:12–13: "Therefore, my beloved, as you have always obeyed, so now, not only as in my presence but much more in my absence, work out your own salvation with fear and trembling; for God is at work in you, both to will and to work for his good pleasure" (rsv). There you have it: *Work out your own salvation—God is at work in you!* No theologian or psychologist has ever lived who can find where man stops and God begins in this relationship.

If the Spirit is the author and sustainer of the Christian's spirituality, why have men like Barth and Bonhoeffer attacked religion as the deepest mark of sin's perverting power? The fullness of references of Barth to the Holy Spirit cannot mean that Barth is attacking spirituality. Rather, he is attacking man-made religion as man makes it in defiance of God's revelation and God's gospel. Religion functions as man's last stronghold against God's revelation and gospel. Bonhoeffer spoke against an introverted piety which could care less for man's suffering, especially during the evil days of Nazi Germany. The more accurate term to define that which Bonhoeffer opposed is religiosity—*Religiosität*. The very manner in which Bonhoeffer kept the church calendar and prayed showed that he had not given up his concern for personal spirituality. If the modern defenders of "secularity" as over against "secularism" evaporate spirituality from their concern, they will become so debilitated that they shall evaporate. The truth of the matter is that those theologians who renounce petitionary prayer (asking and receiving) do so with a guilty conscience; for no sooner have they pronounced such prayer to be sub-Christian than they immediately affirm that they have not crossed prayer out with a big X. We are then told that they most earnestly believe in prayer as meditation, self-analysis, and self-awareness which clarifies the mind, its goals and its motives.

6. *The Holy Spirit and politics.* There is in the Old Testament teaching about the Holy Spirit a close association of the Holy Spirit with government or the "charisma" of governing. When Moses became overburdened with governing, he divided his responsibilities with seventy others. The record makes it manifest that this was also a dividing up of the power of the Holy Spirit given to Moses to rule (Num. 11:16–17). When Moses came to

appoint a successor, he too had to be a man of the Spirit. So Joshua was chosen as a man "full of the Spirit of wisdom" (Deut. 34:9).

The Book of the Judges is the most charismatic book of the Old Testament. The judges were the rulers of Israel between Joshua and the kings. These men were not trained in law or politics or the military. All their diverse skills had to be imparted to them charismatically by the Holy Spirit. This is graphically stated in the phrase "the Holy Ghost fell upon . . . ." In addition to the judges were the kings of Israel who ruled by endowment of the Holy Spirit (1 Sam. 10:6–10, 16:13).

Why do rulers (from Moses through the kings) need a special "political endowment" from the Holy Spirit? Paul tells us that the function of a ruler is to do good (Rom. 13:4). That which a ruler does affects all peoples of his kingdom. Doing good is far more complex and important for a king than for a private citizen. Therefore he needs the help of the Holy Spirit. Consider the following attributes a good ruler must have:

The ruler needs wisdom. The greatness of Solomon was that he saw that as a ruler his need for wisdom overrode his desire for the "goodies" that come with being king. The affairs of the state are wretchedly complex. Only a man with an abundance of wisdom can work his way through such a complexity. Only by wisdom can the right decisions be determined. Therefore, the ruler needs the Holy Spirit that he may be wise above his years, his intelligence, and his education.

The ruler needs character. Again Solomon is the example. Eventually the "goodies" of the kingdom became more important to Solomon than the responsibility of being a wise ruler. In his later days he rotted out—morally. A king needs character to follow the good in all decisions. He needs character to resist the temptations of office. He needs character to resist the abuse of privilege. Only the Holy Spirit can give character adequate to the burdens of kingship.

The ruler needs will power. He may will the good. Can he stick with it? He may be honest in principle. Has he the courage to be honest in fact? He may have character by himself. Can he have character when he is surrounded by pressures of men and of groups? Only from the Spirit of God can ordinary clay receive the will power to be good in the face of all those people and forces that would divert a ruler from his best decisions.

Simply reflect on the history of the kings and their fate in Western Europe. Would the kings of Italy, Spain, France, and Russia be toppled if they were all men and women of the Holy Spirit? Would they yet not be with us if they had ruled by the good in the power of the Holy Spirit? In this light we can understand why in Israel a man had to be a man of the Spirit of God or he did not have the wherewithal to be a good king.

I am not trying, again, to prove too much. I am not interested in creating a political theory of the Holy Spirit. Scripture does not give us that much material. My hope in all of this section was to give some clothing and some concreteness to the idea of Spirit. Ordinarily we think of Spirit as bland, colorless, formless, and ethereal. By seeing all the concrete things he gives to men, I hope to make the Spirit more real and therefore more believable. In this manner I have tried to "bust out" the doctrine of the Holy Spirit. I hope he is more of a person in the mind of the reader than when this section began.

Bibliographical note:

The first theologian I know of who seriously dealt with the full range of the activities of the Spirit is Abraham Kuyper. The importance of his book *The Work of the Holy Spirit* has already been emphasized in earlier notes. Kuyper wrote in 1888. A more recent work which attempts to do some of the things I have done in this chapter is Lindsay Dewar, *The Holy Spirit and Modern Thought*, also referred to in earlier notes.

Heidegger's philosophy contains an attempt to free language from being considered simply a system of signs for the convenient sharing of information and giving it an ontological depth. A book which attempts to do this on other grounds and which is representative of this new approach to language is Leslie Dewart's *Religion, Language and Truth* (New York: Herder and Herder, 1970). The older view he calls the semantical view of language. Language as more personally and "existentially" shaped he calls syntactical language.

The classic works in showing how vast the teleological factors are in the cosmos (separate from biological teleology and later called cosmic teleology) are the two books of L. J. Henderson, *Fitness of the Environment* (New York: Macmillan, 1913) and *Order of Nature* (Cambridge: Harvard University Press, 1917).

A recent modern work covering many more topics and showing that science cannot be understood apart from teleological and holistic considerations is Errol Harris, *The Foundations of Metaphysics in Science*, noted earlier in this chapter. An example of a biologist seeing "spirit" in life in contrast to a purely mechanistic view of life is Edmund Sinnott, *Biology of the Spirit* (New York: Viking Press, 1957).

For rich materials on the relationships of the Divine and human spirit cf. Hendrikus Berkhof, *The Doctrine of the Holy Spirit*, chap. 4, "The Spirit and the Individual." Lindsay Dewar (*The Holy Spirit in Modern Thought*, pt. 4, "The Psychological Aspect") thinks that the closest analogy to the work of the Spirit with people is that of a psychiatrist. Cf. also George S. Hendry, *The Holy Spirit in Christian Theology*, chap. 5, "The Holy Spirit and the Human Spirit," and Arnold B. Come, *Human Spirit and Holy Spirit* (Philadelphia: Westminster, 1959).

12.

The Spirit is the only Sapper

A *sap* is a specially dug trench which zig-zags back and forth so that soldiers can advance to a stronghold and blow it up. The verb *to sap* means to dig such a trench to get near the enemy position. A *sapper* is the name of the soldier who digs such a trench. The word is now used more generally for demolition crews of army engineers who blow up bridges, military installations, and military materiel. These crews are called *sappers*.

A sinner is an entrenched person. Paul uses military language with reference to sinners when he talks about their "strongholds" and "obstacles" (2 Cor. 10:3–4). The sinner is entrenched in unbelief. He is dead in his trespasses and sins. His life is governed by the prince of the power of the air. He is an easy victim of the passions of his flesh and the temptations of the world. He is blind to the truth of God. His mind is at enmity with God, and being fleshly he cannot discern spiritual things. Whatever religion he has he usually uses as a shield against the gospel. When he hears the message of the cross, he calls it foolishness and an offense: "How can any intelligent person believe that?"

The question is then: How is such a man reached? What sort of sapping process will get through his embattlements and blow up his defenses and open him up for faith and the gospel? Using the military language above, the Holy Spirit is the divine sapper who, and who alone, can break up the defenses of the sinner, reach into his entrenchment and destroy it, and bring the truthfulness and the reality of the gospel to bear upon his heart.

To understand the work of the Spirit as the divine sapper it must be understood that the Spirit works through means—Holy

Scripture, the preaching of the gospel, the sacraments, the witnessing of individual Christians, and Christian literature. Furthermore, the Christian does not merely proclaim and say, "Believe it or be damned." A Christian may reason about his faith. If one reads the Book of Acts looking only for those occasions where Paul went to bat for the faith besides preaching it, he will find that many times Paul did just that—went to bat! Furthermore in all of the epistles of the New Testament the writers not only proclaim Christian faith but engage in its defense.

The question to be asked is then: Can the means by themselves get through the sinner's entrenchments so that he comes to faith? As I understand the New Testament, they do not. There are those, of course, who believe that Christianity can be rationally demonstrated and if a man but follow proper reasoning he will come to faith. On the other hand, there are those who say, "Preach the Word and leave the results to the Spirit." I deny both positions. No amount of reasoning separate from the Holy Spirit can demolish the fortresses of unbelief. On the other hand, I believe the Spirit works through all sorts of means, and therefore I do not believe that one preaches the gospel and then sits on his hands.

One of the tragic sides of the history of Christian theology and Christian preaching and witnessing is that the work of the Spirit as one who alone can make the final break-through into the sinner has suffered such poor treatment.

This ambiguity comes out clearly in the status of a Christian philosophy, Christian evidences, and historical faith. Is there such a thing as a Christian philosophy? Is there a philosophy that is the perfect complement to Christianity? Can such a philosophy truly persuade a sinner into saving faith? Are Christian evidences so compelling that a man once informed of them can stay in unbelief only because he is stubborn? Is historical faith the necessary presupposition of saving faith? In all three of these there is frequently the implication that they can shove the sinner over the line into saving faith. However, in the majority of these discussions the precise role of the Spirit is omitted or it remains ambiguous.

No doubt we can put pressure on the sinner by the means we have mentioned. We have not made a forced decision between means or the Holy Spirit. We have asserted means and the Spirit. But we have asserted that the means can never get through without the Spirit. The Spirit alone is the divine sapper that blows up the last defenses of the sinner. Only in this way do men come to faith.

Bringing men to faith only by means has always been a temptation in the church. How wonderful it would be if we could sweetly reason a sinner into faith! But Paul says the unregenerate mind is at enmity with God and cannot perceive spiritual things. How does reason overcome the sinner's profound antipathy to Christian truth? Or does not a thrilling testimony move men's hearts to faith? If we go by thrilling testimonies, which of us can compete with a good mystic LSD trip? More likely the sinner will consider the Christian some sort of psychological oddball. In the twenties and thirties there was a strong movement among American evangelicals to show that the Scriptures were inspired because they anticipated modern science. The heavens of Genesis 1 anticipated modern theory of space, and Hebrews 11:3 anticipated atomic theory. If such anticipations of science could not force modern man to see the truthfulness of Scripture, what else could? Now this apologetical maneuver has lost all its steam because it was gradually recognized that modern science could be found in Scriptures only by torturing the verses to make them say something they did not say.

Paul did say that the gospel was the power of God unto salvation (Rom. 1:16). However, he also adds "to every one who has faith." The power is released only through faith. Then the question surfaces, how do we get the faith to release the power? A person could jump to Romans 10:17 and point out that faith comes from hearing. But again the question surfaces: How does one hear the gospel? In preaching we confront the sinner with the gospel. There is no question that this is the power of God. But what releases a man so that he can hear the gospel in his heart, and what frees a man so that the effects of sin are overcome? Our answer: the divine sapper, the Holy Spirit!

There may be Christians who claim that they were reasoned into faith, or that Christian evidences led them to saving faith, or that the wonderful testimony of a Christian moved them to faith. These means I do not deny. I have already affirmed them. However, the Christian who makes such claims presumes that the Holy Spirit was absent. My thesis is that the only reason that the reasoning or the Christian evidences or the testimony was effective was that the Holy Spirit was silently working with these means. It is certainly not my contention that people are brought to faith only through a set pattern or unimpeachable theological or biblical methods. There is too much rough and tumble and zig and zag to life to claim that. Further, as the old saying goes, "God can strike a hard blow with a crooked stick." My thesis is that the last final wall of the sinner's embattlements is broken through only by the Holy Spirit. He alone can sap that wall and blow it up.

One of the platitudes of logic is that a true theorem can be deduced from a false premise. Natives who boil water to drive out the demons and make it safe to drink unwittingly are practicing the sterilization of water for their own good. Sinners may come a crooked way to faith in Christ, but this does not sanction the crooked way. It means only that the crooked way led inadvertently to Christ just like the natives who unintentionally practiced the purification of water by boiling it.

More light is shed on the work of the Spirit as the divine sapper in Paul's discussion about those who claim to be apostles or teachers. Paul says that he not only wants to know the words that these men say but their power! Why power? Why is power a test for authenticity and apostolicity? The reason is that Christianity is more than a set of religious ideas or a spiritualistic philosophy. It is a gospel which saves. If it is more than a religious philosophy or a spiritual insight on life, it must have power.

Therefore Paul not only wants to know what these professed leaders teach but what kind of power they have in the changing of men's hearts. That is why power was as much a criterion of true Christianity and correct doctrine to Paul. Accordingly he writes: "For the kingdom of God does not consist in talk but in power" (1 Cor. 4:20, RSV).

This is how the Corinthians had become Christians in the first place. Paul said his preaching was in demonstration of the Spirit and power (1 Cor. 2:4). This expression *Spirit and power* means "the Spirit who is a power" or "a powerful Spirit." In 1 Corinthians 1:18 Paul said the gospel was foolishness to those who were perishing so that the gospel was mentally indigestible to the unregenerate. Yet some of the people in Corinth believed this "divine foolishness" (see 1 Cor. 1:25). Paul denies that he won them over by his cleverness or by wisdom or by mind-enchanting oratory. None of these could do the necessary task of sapping the sinner's defenses. It is in this connection that Paul said he got through to the hearts of the Corinthians by "the Spirit and power." Here then is the direct attestation of Paul that the divine sapper is the Holy Spirit and not wisdom, clever speech, or silver-tongued oratory.

Although there are anticipations of the Spirit as the divine Sapper in the history of the church, it was not until the time of the Reformation that it was clearly stated. In his *Small Catechism* Luther wrote:

I believe that I can not, by my own reason or strength, believe in Jesus Christ my Lord, or come to him; but the Holy Ghost has called me through the Gospel, enlightened me in true faith; just as he calls, gathers, enlightens, and sanctifies the whole Christian Church on earth. (Article III)

The famous *Heidelberg Catechism* asks in question 21, "What is true faith?" It answers:

It is not only a certain knowledge whereby I hold for truth all that God has revealed to us in his Word, but also a hearty trust which the Holy Ghost works in me by the Gospel.

It must be said that the first theologian in the history of the church to set out the Holy Spirit as the divine sapper in full theological exposition was John Calvin.[1] In this chapter he examines various alternatives about this task of getting through to the heart of the sinner and convincing him that the gospel is true. He finds that they all come short of achieving such a project. Only the Holy Spirit can, or, more precisely, the witness of the Spirit:

1. *Institutes*, I/7. All Calvin citations are from Battle's translation.

But I reply: the testimony of the Spirit is more excellent than all reason. For as God alone is a fit witness of himself in his Word, so also the Word will not find acceptance in men's hearts before it is sealed by the inward testimony of the Spirit. The same Spirit, therefore, who has spoken through the mouths of the prophets must penetrate into our hearts to persuade us that they faithfully proclaimed what had been divinely commanded (para. 4).

However, Calvin does not think that our belief in the truthfulness of Christianity rests solely on the witness or testimony of the Spirit. The witness of the Spirit is supported by other evidences. These he discusses in chapter 8. Lest a reader be confused as to the order and relationship of the witness of the Spirit and the support of Christian evidences, Calvin said the following:

There are other reasons, neither few nor weak, for which the dignity and majesty of Scripture are not only affirmed in godly hearts, but brilliantly vindicated against the wiles of its disparagers; yet of themselves these are not strong enough to provide a firm faith, until our Heavenly Father, revealing his majesty there, lifts reverence of the Holy Spirit beyond the realm of controversy. Therefore Scripture will ultimately suffice for a saving knowledge of God only when its certainty is founded upon the inward persuasion of the Holy Spirit. Indeed, these human testimonies which exist to confirm it will not be vain, if, as secondary aids to our feebleness, they follow that chief and highest testimony. But those who wish to provide to unbelievers that Scripture is the Word of God are acting foolishly, for only by faith can this be known. Augustine therefore just warns that godliness and peace of mind ought to come first if a man is to understand anything of such great matters.[2]

This citation must be carefully read and pondered over. In my opinion it is the definitive statement of the relationship of God's immediate witness to us in the witness of the Spirit and the function and relationship of human reasoning which supports the truth of Scripture. *Calvin does not rule out means.* He does not believe in the isolated work of the Spirit to lead us into faith. *Means are not sufficient in themselves.* Only the Holy

2. *Institutes*, I/8, para. 13.

Spirit is the divine sapper who destroys the last battlements of the sinner and leads him to faith.

Calvin's statement implies that if we are led to believe by a human persuasion we can be talked out of it. If we are led to believe by God being his own witness in the testimony of the Spirit, we cannot be talked out of it. All rationalistic apologetics which in so many words affirm that Christians are smart because they believe the right "system" and unbelievers are dumb or confused or contradictory because they believe the wrong "system" are built on quicksand. If Christians pretend to be smarter than nonbelievers, there is always the unbeliever who is smarter than Christians (for example, Kant and Hume) who can talk us out of Christianity. The certainty of Christianity is the Holy Spirit. He and he alone is the divine sapper. Beware of counterfeits!

One of Martin Luther's more famous statements was, "The Holy Spirit is no skeptic." He was discussing the importance of theological assertions. A humanistic, mild, tolerant scholar like Erasmus had no appetite for theological debate but was tempted to reduce Christianity to a few moralisms. Luther believed that the Holy Spirit was to bring us truth, not doubt; theology, not a few moralisms; and a bold spirit rather than a hesitant or retiring spirit. This is but another way of expressing the fact that it is the Spirit who makes us believers. The mark of the work of the Spirit is not doubt but full assurance. Let it be emphasized that this certainty Christians possess is not of their ability or the dogmatism of their nature but is the gift of the Holy Spirit.

Another sideline to the assertion that the Holy Spirit is the divine sapper is to be found in Romans 8:26–27. In this passage Paul says that we do not know how we should pray because of our weakness. From verse 18 on, his theme has been the "bondage to decay" of this present life and how we Christians groan under its burden waiting for the day of redemption. Part of this bondage is our weakness when it comes to knowing how to pray. Paul says it is the Spirit who remedies this weakness and offers up for us prayers that are acceptable to God. Only the Spirit—I repeat, only the Spirit—can overcome that bondage and weakness! And so it is with our entire Christian experience. From the day of the birth of faith in our hearts to the last spiritual act we do on earth, it is all by, with, and through the Spirit who alone is the power of God over our sinfulness, our weakness, and our depravity.

One final word. It has been charged that the emphasis by Luther and Calvin on the Holy Spirit in aiding the sinner coming to faith really undermines man's own role in religious experience. What are such critics reading? At least from my reading of all the great emphasis on faith by Luther and Calvin, I get the impression that they are deeding over to man exactly that which is his. Which of these two men ever claimed that God vicariously believed for man? Or that the Holy Spirit ever took away from man that which man could do on his own?

It is perhaps for this reason that Pentecostal theologians, writers, and preachers were testy about the historic doctrine of the witness of the Spirit which one thought they would accept with acclaim. They do in their own way, but they are suspicious that it is a species of Calvinism, and their theology is Arminian; or that it is really a theology of the Word and not of the Spirit; or that it had too many doctrinal complications which inhibit the true spontaneity of the Spirit.[3]

We need to blow the whistle here! Do Pentecostal theologians really understand the Reformers' doctrine of the witness of the Spirit? Have they worked meticulously with the texts as the Lutheran and Reformed theologians have? Have they not gone the fatal step and substituted the objectively grounded witness of the Spirit in history and Scripture with a psychological, enthusiastic, and subjective version? Is there not a need in the Pentecostal movement to come to terms with historical theology and academically responsible biblical exegesis?

---

3. Cf. Walter J. Hollenweger, *The Pentecostals* (London: SCM Press, 1972).

Bibliographical note:

As indicated in the exposition, the classic historical passage on the
Spirit as the One who breaks through man's depravity to reach his
heart with the gospel is John Calvin's *Institutes of the Christian Religion,* I/7. I have attempted to update the entire discussion as the
doctrine of the witness of the Spirit has had such an uneven history
in my book *The Witness of the Spirit* (Grand Rapids: Eerdmans,
1959). That book contains a selected bibliography for any reader interested in more detailed research of this topic. For a treatment of the
witness of the Spirit with a different focus from mine, cf. George
Hendry, *The Holy Spirit in Christian Theology,* chap. 4, "The Holy
Spirit and the Word."

13.

The Hermes from heaven

Greek religion was rich with gods, goddesses, and mythology. Furthermore, in the passage of the centuries the gods underwent many changes of significance and representation. Hermes was such a god. At one state in his transit from function to function he was considered the messenger of the gods to men and the interpreter of their messages. From the name Hermes the Greeks formed a verb *hermēneuō,* "I interpret." From the verb they derived a noun which translated into English comes across as "hermeneutics." Hermeneutics means the art and skill of interpretation.

One of the claims of the Reformers was that the Holy Spirit helps the believer to understand the Word of God. If Calvin was great for developing the doctrine of the witness of the Spirit, Luther was great for developing the doctrine of the role of the Holy Spirit in the interpretation of Scripture. This he did in his famous reply to Erasmus, *The Bondage of the Will* (1525). The purpose of the interpretation of Scripture is to make the Scripture clear. To Luther there was an outer and an inner clarity of Scripture. By the usual laws or rules of language, a Christian could understand the Scripture as a written document. This is the external clarity of Scripture. Due to man's sinfulness he needs an inward assist so that he might grasp the spiritual Word of God as the Word of God. The Word of God is a spiritual entity and can only be understood in faith with the help of the Holy Spirit. This is the inner clarity of Scripture. Hence, to Luther the Holy Spirit was the Hermes from heaven.

There is scriptural support for this. John writes: "But the

anointing [of the Holy Spirit] which you received from him abides in you, and you have no need that any one should teach you; as his anointing [by his Spirit] teaches you about everything, and is true, and is no lie, just as it [the Spirit] has taught you, abide in him" (1 John 2:27, RSV).

The very academic scholar trained in the interpretation of ancient texts is not happy with this concept of the Holy Spirit being the Hermes from heaven. How, specifically, concretely, does the Holy Spirit help a biblical scholar interpret the Bible? What detectable difference can one show between the interpretation of the scholar who claims no reliance on the Holy Spirit and one who claims reliance on the Holy Spirit? Is there really any cash value in the traditional doctrine of the illumination of the Spirit?

Let us first scrape the plate clean. The Holy Spirit as the Hermes from heaven does not mean that Christians understand the Scriptures out of the blue with no regard to Luther's view of the external clarity of Scripture. The illumination of the Spirit is no prayer-meeting substitute for the hard work of learning Hebrew and Greek and using the standard lexicons, commentaries, and other research materials. I make no defense for a minister who does not study the technical and grammatical aspects of a text but stands behind the pulpit, opens his mouth, and expects the Holy Spirit to fill it. If this is the case, it casts grave doubts on the divine attributes of the Spirit when measured against what is said.

To show how the Holy Spirit is the Hermes from heaven, let us start with Kierkegaard's *For Self-Examination*.[1] In this book Kierkegaard poses the question how a lover reads a love letter from his lover when they happen to speak two different languages. The first thing the lover must do with the letter is to translate it. He gets out his dictionary of the foreign language—perhaps even a grammar—and goes to work. He translates it word by word, line by line, paragraph by paragraph, until the entire translated letter is on the desk before him.

But doing all that hard work of translating that letter into his language is not to read the letter as a love letter. Now that he

---

1. Søren Kierkegaard, *For Self-Examination and Judge for Yourselves* (New York: Oxford, 1941).

has the complete translation he relaxes, leans back in his chair, and reads the translated letter as a love letter.

So it is with Holy Scripture. We cannot avoid all the hard work of looking up Hebrew and Greek words, puzzling over constructions, consulting commentaries, and other such helps. But doing this careful academic job of translating and interpreting Scripture is not to read the Word of God as the Word of God. Unfortunately that is where the professor stops. But to read Scripture as the Word of God he must read it the second time. Now it is no longer an academic task but it is a case of letting God's Word get through to man's soul *as God's Word*. It is in the second reading of the letter that the Holy Spirit, the Hermes from heaven, enters into the process of understanding Holy Scripture.

Kierkegaard gives us a second illustration. A little boy is to be spanked by his father. While the father goes for the rod the boy stuffs the bottom of his pants with several table napkins. When the father returns and administers the whipping the boy feels no pain as the napkins absorb the whack of the rod. The little boy represents the biblical scholars. They pad their britches with their lexicons, commentaries, and concordances. As a result the Scripture never reaches them as the Word of God. Having nullified its power by shielding themselves with their academic paraphernalia, they thus never hear the Scriptures as the Word of God. If they would unpack their books from their britches (which are necessary rightfully used, as illustrated in the story of the love letter) then the Scriptures could get through to them as the Word of God. Allowing Holy Scripture to get through to us as the Word of God is the special work of the Holy Spirit.

A second factor in understanding the Holy Spirit as the Hermes from heaven is the change that has taken place in the understanding of documents in general and Holy Scripture in particular. The two men who pioneered in this direction were Schleiermacher and Dilthey.

Any work of art—painting, building, musical score, play, or work of literature—was done by a human being for human beings. In order to understand such products and so interpret them, the human dimension cannot be eliminated without causing distortion. Strict grammatical, lexical, historical, critical interpretation eliminates this personal element and therefore comes short of a true understanding of what is being interpreted. To that degree then the interpretation is a falsification.

In more recent language the interpreter must be able to identify or relate with the painting or the sculpture or the music or the piece of literature. The critical work is not to be bypassed, even as Kierkegaard insisted that it should not. But critical interpretation or exegesis of human products which attempt to say something come short of the mark. The interpreter must reckon with the psychological dimension of what he is interpreting.

Such products of man which intend to say something are life-expressions. They are external expressions of an internal emotion or conviction or perspective on life. The interpreter has to try his best to catch this life-expression or this personal interpretation of a part of reality or of a universal human experience. All the grammatical studies in the world cannot build this bridge between the interpreter and what is being interpreted.

It takes sympathy, empathy, rapport, understanding in depth in contrast to technical understanding. It is the difference between understanding something and explaining something. Problems in mathematics or logic or chemistry are explained. Works of art can only be understood. That is the basic reason so few scientists are ever poets or poets are ever scientists.

To touch base for a moment, let us remind ourselves that the critical treatment of the text is the explanation of the text— Luther's external clarity. The understanding of the text as the Word of God is Luther's internal clarity.

This can be illustrated so many different ways. People who have no sense of the artistic or beautiful race through an art gallery for the sole reason of being able to say they have been through it. A lover of art may stand before a painting for an hour in order to drink in all he possibly can from the picture. One impressionistic painter had his painting spit upon all day long for this was the way the public tramping through the museum reacted to the painting. Each night the janitor had to wipe the spit off the picture. The common herd did not have the capacity to understand the artist.

The same is true in history. The positivistic study of history is a fakery. An impersonal, objective, detached explanation of the story of human beings, rich in personality traits, is a phony one.

If there were no psychological bridge between the historian and history, the historian would not know what to write about. If he calls himself a strict positivistic historian he is unaware of the fact that he uses a great deal of psychological insight to understand the history he is writing about. If the positivist historian were to succeed he would have *Hamlet* without Hamlet, and hence a series of hit-and-miss conversations and bits of action but no play or no drama.

Science too has its subjective side. In typical introductory books for college freshmen and sophomores the scientific method is set out as if it were a completely impersonal, humanly detached procedure. We now know better. The experimenter cannot avoid putting a lot of himself into his scientific research.

Back to the issue: how does the Holy Spirit, the Hermes from heaven, make a real difference in biblical interpretation? All we have said in the above paragraphs has pointed up two facts: (1) in the realm of human products, especially those which intend to say something or express something, a purely critical, objective approach is not enough to interpret the subject matter adequately; (2) an unavoidable psychological or personal dimension must be added to the attempt at interpretation in order for a complete and adequate interpretation to be made. The more the interpreter can catch the emotions, the intuitions, and the life expressions of the original artist or writer the better his interpretation will be.

It is the Holy Spirit who gives the Christian interpreter of Holy Scripture that subjective disposition, that sense of harmony with the mind of the Author of Scripture that enables him to better interpret Scripture. This does not eliminate the critical study of Scripture, let alone being substitute for it. But the critical, grammatical, and historical interpretation of Scripture comes short of the full understanding of Scripture.

If Kierkegaard, Schleiermacher, and Dilthey are correct, then strict scientific biblical interpretation comes short of the full understanding of Scripture. The Holy Spirit is necessary for the understanding of that added human, personal, psychological— yes, even existential—dimension. The Holy Spirit does make a material difference in biblical interpretation.

A look at literature may help clarify the point. Milton lost a close friend when Edward King drowned in the Irish sea. To express his loss he wrote his great memorial poem *Lycidas*. A student may trace down all the references to ancient mythology in the poem and all the references to contemporary events in Milton's life expressed in the poem, and the history and etymology of the more important words. But unless he has lost a very dear friend in a tragic death there is a dimension of the poem that will escape him. He can master the outer clarity of the poem but not the inner clarity.

It is well known that Milton suffered another tragedy in that he went blind in the midst of his career. He expressed his feelings in a *Sonnet on his Blindness*. Once again, a Ph.D. candidate may ferret out all the technicalities about the poem. But unless in some way he has been suddenly crippled or debilitated the real pathos of the poem will escape him. A person in a wheelchair may not know much of English literature but he will immediately know how Milton felt, for that is the way he feels. A singer who gets cancer of the larynx or a violin player who has a hand crushed or a scientist who has a brain tumor which has robbed his mind of its clarity and powers will each know in his own way what Milton is trying to say.

In the study of Scripture it is the ministry of the Holy Spirit to give us that subjectivity necessary to understand Scripture. It is the Spirit who puts us in rapport with the Father so that we may understand his mind as it is revealed in Scripture. It is the Spirit who helps give us those kinds of human intuitions which unlock the feelings and the mental set of the authors of Scripture.

Granted, there is something elusive about this work of the Spirit. But this quality is not unique to Scripture. If Schleiermacher, Kierkegaard, and Dilthey are correct, it is true of all interpretation. There is a necessary psychological dimension required for adequate interpretation but that dimension is elusive and cannot be gotten out into the open, i.e., objectified.

Again let us turn to art to see how this is so, namely, that some quality that is elusive, intangible, and incapable of objectification is nevertheless an indispensable part of adequate interpretation. Some art critics think Picasso's *Guernica* is the greatest painting of the twentieth century. Supposing two different people are looking at it. The first is a physicist who has spent his life with mathematics, working in a science lab, and reading his technical journals and books. He knows nothing of the history of painting in the past one hundred years nor of Picasso nor anything but the vaguest details of the civil war in Spain in the thirties. As he looks at the *Guernica* with its misshapen horses and men, the odd way people are "stuck" in the picture, the grotesque faces of men and of beasts, the bizarre way the painting is put together, he thinks it the work of a madman. He mutters to himself about typical off-beat, schizophrenic artists of our times. What a relief to get back to the order and sanity of his lab! The physicist lacks all the subjectivity necessary to understand the *Guernica*.

The second person looking at the *Guernica* is a Spanish artist. He knows the history of the development of Picasso's style. This is not the only kind of picture like this Picasso has painted. He knows what the development of the camera has done to the painter. He knows the story of the terrible bombing of the little Spanish town of Guernica. He himself lived through the Spanish civil war. He finally turns away from the picture weeping. The picture has moved him deeply. Why? Because he has had the subjectivity really to see what the picture is saying. Knowing his Picasso and his Spanish history, he is therefore able through this subjectivity to get a response from the picture that reduces him to tears.

How can you get this subjectivity out into the open? How can you count it and measure it? How can you treat it like a Greek verb or the history of some Greek philosophical concept? It just can't be done. Yet that subjectivity is necessary to understand the *Guernica* if it is to be more than one mad jumble of men and horses. This "subjectivity" is so "objective" that without it the *Guernica* cannot be understood. No "objectivist" will leave the picture in tears.

Is it not the same with Holy Scripture? Do we not have "physicists" in biblical interpretation? The major criticism of the famous *International Critical Commentary* produced during the heyday of religious liberalism was that so many of its volumes were devoted almost entirely to emending the text, noting grammatical constructions, attempting to show the development of religion in Israel, and scouting the religions contemporary with the biblical book for possible sources of the materials in the book. One looked in vain for interpretations with meaning, depth, insight, and understanding. How could it be there if the commentary was written by a "biblical physicist"? Completely engrossed in the technicalities of linguistic and historical scholarship as he was, the interpreter did not have the subjectivity to grasp the meaning of the book and so give it a just interpretation. Unfortunately, "biblical physicists" did not die out with the *International Critical Commentary* but are still alive today in substantial numbers.

When a person is born of the Spirit and is so indwelt by the Spirit, he has (as we cited Calvin in the previous section) the same Spirit which inspired Holy Scripture. He has the subjectivity necessary to understand Scripture—the kind of subjectivity Kierkegaard, Schleiermacher, and Dilthey talked about. But one can no more get this subjectivity out into the open and make it an objectivity than one can get out into the open the subjectivity necessary to understand the *Guernica*.

Let us consider a comment made by Werner Elert in his yet untranslated work *The Christian Faith*.[2]

Elert was one of the great Lutheran scholars of this century. His work was of such stature that Barth made it the subject matter of one of his seminars. In this work Elert says that even though Luther and Calvin did not have all the technical equipment available to a modern biblical scholar, they understood the New Testament better than modern scholars. This is no Pietist or Fundamentalist speaking who wants to give modern critical scholarship a knife between the ribs. He is a German professor with a substantial reputation for scholarship. Don't overlook the enormity of the claim. A pyramid of materials have been developed since the days of Luther and Calvin to help the interpreter of Scripture. Then why such a claim?

Elert made the claim because he believed that in spirit, in heart, in pulsebeat, in rapport of mind to mind, Luther and Calvin were closer to the New Testament writers than modern, highly trained, technically skilled New Testament interpreters. Luther and Calvin had that elusive nonobjectifiable subjectivity which is absolutely imperative for the understanding of a document that led them directly to the heart of the meaning of the

2. *Der christliche Glaube,* 5th ed. (Hamburg: Furche Verlag, 1960).

New Testament. Modern scholars with all their technicalities but without this requisite subjectivity (in an expression borrowed from Leo XIII) "gnaw the bark of Scripture" but never get to its pith.

This is the sense in which the Holy Spirit is the Hermes from heaven. He can give that "divine subjectivity" that puts the heart in harmony with the Word of God. If there must be not only a critical, grammatical, and historical bridge built between the interpreter and that which is interpreted, but also a psychological or "life-expression" or existential bridge, then the same is true in scriptural interpretation. We do not deny a measure of truth in what Bultmann says when he asserts we must have some sort of preconditioning ("preunderstanding") before we can really grasp a subject matter, and therefore there must be some sort of under-standing of life, pain, guilt, a sense of the infinite, a sense of per-sonal meaning, a striving for truth and reality, and so on, that is necessary for coming to terms with the gospel. But the deepest subjectivity necessary for fully understanding the inspired text is to be guided by the Spirit who inspired the text. He is not only the Author of an inspired Scripture, but he is also the Hermes from heaven who leads us into the fullest depths of its meaning and gives us that "divine subjectivity" which puts us on the same wave length as the Divine Author of Scripture. Perhaps this "divine subjectivity," as elusive as it is to make concrete, is the greatest objectivity necessary in understanding the heart of Scripture.

Bibliographical notes:

For a thorough explanation of the history of hermeneutics from Barth to the New Hermeneutic, with dips into history as well as detailed explanation of technical vocabulary, see James Robinson, "Hermeneutic since Barth," in James M. Robinson and John B. Cobb, eds., *The New Hermeneutic: New Frontiers in Theology*, vol. 2 (New York: Harper & Row, 1964), pp. 1–77. Kierkegaard's *For Self-Examination and Judge for Yourselves* is especially valuable for his discussion on how to read the Bible as the Word of God. For showing how much the scientist contributes to the so-called "objectivity" of the scientific method, the modern classic is Michael Polyani, *Personal Knowledge* (New York: Harper, Torchbooks, 1958). Elert's claim about the Reformers will be found in his untranslated work *Der christliche Glaube* referred to earlier in this chapter. R. G. Collingwood, *The Idea of History* (Oxford: Clarendon Press, 1946) is frequently appealed to as a refutation of the "cult of objectivity" in history, as if historians could extract the human element in history and write it as if it were a science. Its goal was "to tell it as it exactly happened" [Ranke: *wie es eigentlich gewesen*].

It must be mentioned that reference to Hermes occurs in the New Testament. When Paul and Barnabas were at Lystra and healed the man with the crippled feet, the natives in their excitement called Barnabas Zeus, as he was apparently the leader of the team, but they called Paul Hermes, as he was the chief [hence, eloquent] speaker—the voice of the gods to man. Cf. Acts 14:8–12.

For those who wish an explanation of Picasso and the *Guernica* we suggest *Horizon*, 7:65–79, Winter 1965.

14.

Can a bodyless, sexless Spirit love?

It comes as a surprise that the New Testament frequently associates the Holy Spirit with love (Rom. 5:5, 15:30, 1 Cor. 6:6, Gal. 5:22, Col. 1:8, 2 Tim. 1:7).

Ordinarily when we think of love—apart from banal, overworked clichés that God is love—we think of it in terms of a human body. We imagine a beautiful face on a woman or a handsome face on a man. We think of the general pleasing bodily shape and the sex organs that mark out the male and the female. We are excited when we think of the act of love itself with the maximum excitement of not only the pleasure zones but the whole psyche.

But what can love mean to a creature that is bodyless and without sexual organs? How can a Spirit love? It is not easy to imagine. But we can make some headway in spite of our earthly limitations.

Back to the Trinity! In the doctrine of the Trinity we mentioned the mystery—and God help the theologian who won't let the doctrine of the Trinity rest as a mystery—of three *personae* and one *substance*. Whatever may be said about a *persona*, a *persona* is at least personal. And if a *persona* is at least personal, he can love. The Holy Spirit is therefore as much capable of loving as are the Father and the Son. If we then think of the Holy Spirit as a *persona* we should have no trouble thinking of him as loving.

In recent times scholars have analyzed the different meanings of love in the Greek language as *storgē, philia, erōs* and *agapē*. We shall concentrate on the difference between *erōs* and *agapē*, duly bowing to the scholar's observation that this is an over-simplification!

Erōs means self-centered, self-gratifying love, and refers to purely human love or the kind of love manifest among the Olympian gods and goddesses. *Agapē* is the special kind of love revealed in the New Testament. The highest expression of this love is God's gift of his Son as a sacrifice for the sins of the world on the cross. It is divine, sacrificial, outgoing, spiritual love.

Granted the oversimplification in the above, we can neverthe-less think of examples of love that are not erotic. Platonic love between a woman and a man, for example, is a relationship sustained in terms of attractiveness of personalities rather than of bodies. There can be a man-to-man and a woman-to-woman love that is *agapē* love and therefore not homosexual and there-fore not erotic. Well-known biblical examples are the love be-tween David and Jonathan and between Naomi and Ruth.

If love can be made spiritual and cut loose from its center in the erotic then it takes no great leap of the mind to understand that a Spirit can love. If a man can love a man in *agapē* love; and if a man can love a woman with *agapē* (platonic) love; and if a woman can love a woman with *agapē* love; and if a woman can love a man with *agapē* love—then the Holy Spirit can love! And then the Holy Spirit can instill in us the love of God (Rom. 5:5)! Yes, a bodyless, sexless, eroticless Spirit can have *agapē* love, and can inspire *agapē* love! (Even the Freudian con-cept that man cannot have *agapē* love without a trace of some erotic love does not refute the above, but merely stresses man's limitations and his sinnerhood).

Part of the problem in theology of Western Protestants and in understanding the relationship of the Spirit to love is that as Protestants we are in the tradition of a theology of faith. This stems from the Reformation where justification by faith played such an enormous role. There may have been a theology of love before Augustine but he certainly made it the character of his theology and much of the subsequent theology of the Middle Ages. The cities of man and of God in the *City of God* are differ-entiated by their two different kinds of love. The supreme mark of the elect is that they love God. Perhaps the greatest theologian of love in the history of theology was Peter Abelard (1079–1142).

Roman Catholic theology has been profoundly influenced by Galatians 5:6—faith working by love! Granted, faith is the initiatory virtue whereby we are saved but love is the supreme virtue. The theology of Roman Catholicism is far more marked by the importance of love than is Protestantism with its continued emphasis on justification by faith, the life of faith, and "trusting" God for everything.

Protestantism could stand a strong infusion of the doctrine of love in the heart of its theology as well as in its ethics. The notion that the Spirit can love might then not be so hard to imagine. Certainly when Paul speaks of the gifts of the Spirit in 1 Corinthians 12–14 he says that the greatest gifts are faith, hope, and love and that the greatest of these is love! And love is a charismatic gift of the Spirit. Yes, the bodyless Spirit can love!

An interesting sidelight in philosophical theology arises here. So many books are concerned with proving the existence of God, or debating that talk about God is meaningful and not nonsense. But what if Pascal is right? that only those who love God truly know him! What if the reality of God is known only in love? Or what if Augustine is right when he affirms that we only truly know what we truly love? If this is the case, then all the theistic proofs are academic confetti. It is like trying to prove roses are beautiful by locating their electromagnetic vibrations on the electromagnetic spectrum (measured in angstrom units). Or it is like trying to prove a voice is beautiful by watching its pattern on an oscilloscope—something a deaf person could do!

Is not the entire God-problem to be rethought if God is known by those who love him and not by those who think correctly about him?

A great philosophical tradition almost three thousand years old has been carried on by some of the greatest of human minds about God, his attributes, and his purposes. This John Cardinal Newman argued in his book *The Idea of a University*. His thesis was that any institution which claimed to teach universal knowledge and left out the question of God, one of the most universal questions of the human race, was not truly a university. This tradition we would not minimize. We are suggesting that it has been over-rationalized and overphilosophized. If the Spirit is a Spirit of love, and God is love, we feel a dimension has been left out of such discussion, giving it a stuffy academic atmosphere for the lungs and a paper taste for the tongue. If the Spirit can love and creates love for God, perhaps there is a shorter, clearer, more blessed way to the reality of God than via theistic proofs and Christian evidences.

Bibliographical notes:

The greatest treatise on love in the twentieth century is that of Anders Nygren, *Agape and Eros* (Philadelphia: Westminster, 1953). Cf. also Gottfried Quell and Ethelbert Staufer, *"agapaō"* et al. in *Theological Dictionary of the New Testament*, 1:21–54. Abelard as the greatest theologian of love is expounded by Richard E. Weingart, *The Logic of Divine Love* (Oxford: Clarendon Press, 1971). The interpretation of Augustine's theology as a theology of love is to be found in John Burnaby, *Amor Dei: A Study of the Religion of St. Augustine* (London: Hodder and Stoughton, 1938). For the Greek philosophical of *erōs* see F. E. Peters, *Greek Philosophical Terms: A Historical Lexicon* (New York: New York University Press, 1967). Barth attempts to recoup love for Protestant theology in his treatment of the attributes (or, perfections) of God in *Church Dogmatics*, II/1, sec. 28, "The Being of God Who Loves in Freedom." The modern theologian who persisted most in his conviction that God's love would conquer all, hence universalism, was Nels Ferré, *The Christian Understanding of God* (New York: Harper and Brothers, 1951). For a literary, psychological study of love cf. C. S. Lewis, *The Four Loves* (London: Fontana Books, 1960). It is distressing that most of the above materials either omit the relationship of the Spirit to love or provide only sparse comments on it.

One delightful variation to this is Jonathan Edwards, *Treatise on Grace* (Greenwood, S.C.: The Attic Press, 1971). Edwards identifies the Holy Spirit with the love of God. The book also strongly defends the personality of the Spirit for fear that the traditional doctrine of the Trinity might undermine it unintentionally.

15.

The situation is fluid

Those of us alive during World War II were astounded at Hitler's amazing speed in conquering his enemies. When he turned upon Russia it appeared as if nothing could stop his tanks until they reached Moscow. Suddenly the reports from the front took an odd turn. The radio announced strategic withdrawals which stunned the enemy. Although speculation arose that the Nazi armies had retreated to regroup so as to launch a crushing blow to the Russians, it was not hard to decode what was beginning to happen. Then came the announcement: "The situation is fluid." It meant that the Russians were advancing at such a rate and the Nazis retreating at such a rate that any such idea of a "front line" or "line of combat" became meaningless. The indefinable mass of advancing Russians and retreating Nazis could only be described by saying that "the situation is fluid."

A lot of things in theology can be described with those same words: "the situation is fluid." God acts in his sovereignty as God and yet man acts in his spontaneity as God's creature in the image of God. Who knows where God's sovereignty ends and man's spontaneity begins? The situation is fluid!

We all want a God who is there when we need him! We want a God who answers prayer in a realistic way. Yet the spiritual dimension of prayer must be preserved to save prayer from being disguised magic or superstition. When does God's action in prayer end and our spiritual response begin? The situation is fluid!

Scripture says that within the heart of the believer is also the Holy Spirit. Romans 8:16 indicates that there is commerce between God's Spirit and our spirit. But what do we do under the leadership of God's Spirit and at the same time under the motivations of our own spirit? The Holy Spirit does not emerge in our consciousness as clearly as tables, apples, and trees. Nor are the well-springs of our own action equally as clear. "The situation is fluid."

Into our consciousness all sorts of things tumble. At times it is not unlike a child's box of toys that has had the toys tossed into it with no sense of order whatsoever. We do not have the clearness of mind to know out of that tumble of events what is of the Spirit and what is our own doing except that both are there! Scripture tells us that!

Again, psychologists tell us all sorts of things about our unconscious, subconscious, and preconscious mind. There are things at the focal point of our attention and things dimly perceived at the periphery. There are things that boil up into our consciousness whose origin is unknown to us. Then there are the vast caverns of our memory. With all our advancement in psychology, nobody as yet has written so eloquently nor so perceptively about memory as Augustine in his *Confessions*. Yet, according to the New Testament, God's Spirit and our spirit are at work in all of this. The situation is certainly fluid!

But though it may be fluid it is not chaotic. Paul lists for us the works of the flesh (Gal. 5:19–21). No Christian has the right to call a work of the flesh a deed of the Spirit. Paul also lists the fruit of the Spirit in contrast to the flesh (Gal. 5:22–24), and no man can list a fruit of the Spirit among the evil works of the flesh. We certainly know where some things come from. God does not tempt anybody, declares James (James 1:13), and no man can say Jesus is cursed with the help of the Holy Spirit (1 Cor. 12:3).

In between these clearly marked works of the flesh and works of the Spirit are many uncharted waters. The Christian cannot prevent himself from sailing in these waters. And in these waters "the situation is fluid."

If this is the case, certain lessons should be learned. The first is that Christians should recognize the complexity of the relationship of the divine Spirit to the human spirit. How sad it is when this complexity is not known nor understood. We cannot with certainty label certain things as stemming from God's Spirit and other things as the doings of our own spirit. Things do not emerge in our consciousness with sufficient clarity to make such distinctions.

A Christian borders on arrogance when he so easily and readily identifies something in his experience as of the Spirit of God when it is no more than a hunch or feeling that he has. The life of faith means that we persist in the Christian life when the situation is fluid and obscure! Real faith confesses ignorance as readily as it confesses light. How else can we live when the situation is fluid?

The second lesson follows from the first. We should always speak about the Spirit in humility. When sin is sin and righteousness is righteousness, we may speak with certainty. However, when the situation is fluid and we cannot tell what is of the divine Spirit and what is of the human spirit we must speak with humility. To lack humility means we do not understand that the situation is fluid; or, that we attempt to dogmatize faith into sight by affirming with no definable evidence that something is of the Holy Spirit.

Furthermore, no Christian should so speak as to put other Christians in the position of fighting God. No Christian wishes to fight God. When another Christian brazenly says "The Holy Spirit told me—" then to oppose the opinion of that Christian is to resist the Holy Spirit. Humility and loving regard for the rights of other Christians ought to restrain us from such easy identifications of our opinions with the mind of the Spirit. Only apostles and prophets are inspired.

The belief that the situation is fluid is not a denial of the activity of the Spirit. It is an assertion that as Christians knowing Holy Scripture we cannot evenso readily identify that which the Holy Spirit does and that which our spirit inaugurates. There is a conjunction here of the divine Spirit and human spirit that no man can bring clearly into focus nor for which he can find the lines of demarcation. That which the Spirit does is known from the clarity of the New Testament and not by what we can decipher from our own experience. But that is where the rub is! Too many enthusiastic Christians claim to be able accurately to decode their experiences. If the situation is truly fluid, then no such deciphering of the work of the Spirit in our experiences is possible. The most intense emotion cannot force faith into sight.

We live by faith and no more clearly than that situation where we believe the Spirit is at work but recognize the situation as fluid.

We may be mixed up another way. We may presume that the Holy Spirit is working when he is not. Christians, with all the human race, have great capacities for self-deception.

There are also situations where it goes beyond our powers to assess whether the Spirit is leading people or not. Virgins have committed suicide rather than submit to rape. Soldiers have committed suicide for fear that if taken alive they will be tortured into betraying their army. People have committed suicide to escape an excruciating, painful death or a death of terrible attrition and helplessness. The situation is fluid. Moral principles and mercy struggle with each other. We can neither make the situation clear by dogmatizing nor by becoming excessively emotional. Only God knows the truth when the situation is this fluid. Here again we need not despair, for greater than our thoughts and our wisdom is the wisdom of the Holy Spirit. And we walk by faith in that wisdom when our own minds are numb.

Bibliographical note:

Augustine's unsurpassed description of memory will be found in *Confessions*, X/8–11. His affirming that the city of God lies mixed up with the city of man, illustrating that the "situation is fluid," will be found in the *City of God*, XI/1: "[the city of God and the city of man] are in this present world commingled, and as it were, entangled together."

16.

Prof, you have to answer it in this lecture!

Our great modern universities had very humble origins. The basic pattern in the beginning was that a noted authority on a certain subject would receive fees or tuition from students and in turn would lecture to them on his specialty. However, the ground rules were loose and apparently many professors took advantage of the lax situation. The students naturally became angry so they set up rules that the professors had to abide by if they were to keep receiving tuition fees. One such rule was that the professor could not give too much time in a given course dishing out irrelevant, introductory materials. Another rule was that he could not be absent from the city for any period of time without consent of the tuition-paying students. The rule which catches our interest at this point was that a professor could not tell a student that the important question he asked him would be answered in a future lecture. An important question had to be answered in the lecture in which it was asked.

Until this day there are reasons why professors will say to a student's question, "We will answer that question in a later lecture." One reason is that the professor may feel that the question is so controversial that his answer is going to make many of the students angry with him. The delayed answer then turns out to be a dodge and the question never gets answered. To cut off the dodge the students in the earlier situation demanded important questions be answered in the lecture period asked.

So I am caught! A great band of fervent evangelicals believe that besides the work of the Holy Spirit in regeneration, there is a second work of the Spirit known as the baptism of the Spirit.

Furthermore, the sign that informs the believer that he has received this second work of grace or this baptism of the Spirit is that he speaks in tongues.

Lest the Pentecostal reader fear that we have not done our homework in Pentecostal theology and given it a fair shake, let him be assured that among many the works we have given special attention to are the doctrinal section of Bloch-Hoell's *The Pentecostal Movement* (New York: Humanities Press, 1964) as well as the much lengthier doctrinal discussion in Hollenweger's *The Pentecostals,* referred to in an earlier chapter. We have also read the *Statement of Fundamental Truths* of the General Council of the Assemblies of God.

There are differences among Pentecostals. One of the merits of Bloch-Hoell's book is that it is a truly international study of Pentecostalism. Written as an analysis of Scandinavian Pentecostalism, it was reviewed so favorably that a second edition was written in English and expanded to include the American Pentecostal movement. In passing it reveals the divergences among the Pentecostals. Evidently many of the early Pentecostals believe in three works of the Spirit: regeneration, sanctification, and baptism in the Spirit. The movement has tended to absorb the second into the third and speak only of two works of the Spirit.

The common denominator of the Pentecostals' unique doctrine of the Spirit is as follows:

1. In addition to the work of the Spirit in regenerating men by faith in Christ, the Spirit also baptizes Christians as a distinct separate act apart from their salvation.

2. This baptism in the Spirit does not come automatically with regeneration but must be sought in a serious and diligent manner. The "blessedness" or purpose of it is power for living the Christian life and spreading the gospel.

3. The unique and necessary "physical" sign is that those who receive the second blessing of the Spirit speak in foreign tongues *(xenolalia).* "Physical" means "an immediate supernatural manifestation to the senses."

The basic difference between the general run of the great historic Protestant traditions and Pentecostal theology is that the historic traditions believe that all major blessings are received at the time of justification and regeneration. The Pentecostal the-

ology, to the contrary, divides the church up into those regenerated and those regenerated and baptized by the Spirit.

Dear professor, in this lecture give your verdict! My verdict
is that the Church of Christ, the body of believers, is one church
in its blessings and cannot be so divided up.

First, let us list our agreements. Bloch-Hoell's analysis reveals
that at all major points of doctrine the Pentecostals are one with
historic Christianity or evangelical theology. Both the historic
traditions and Pentecostal theology teach that a man is not a
Christian without regeneration and that all Christians have the
Holy Spirit (John 3:3, Rom. 8:9).

Furthermore, both traditions teach that the Holy Spirit is the
source of power for leading the Christian life and for effectively
carrying out the Great Commission.

The student of the history of theology knows that Luther and
Calvin were profound students of the Holy Spirit. John Calvin
has been called *the theologian* of the Holy Spirit.

How does an evangelical committed to basically the Reformed
theology assess the unique claim of Pentecostal theology?

1. The literature of Pentecostalism impresses us that it is yet
more of a movement than a mature, competent theological tradition. Bloch-Hoell writes that "the Pentecostal Movement did not
develop any scholarly theology during the first sixty years of its
existence" (p. 97). The contrast of the Pentecostal Movement
with the Reformation is enormous. Most of the Reformers were
scholars, professors, and doctors of theology. It is not contested
that Luther and Calvin were both highly educated men, geniuses
in their own right. Their literary output was enormous and of a
profound nature. In not the slightest measure do the Pentecostal
leaders manifest the same theological and biblical erudition of
the Reformers.

2. The body of Christ is one. We cite only one of many
possible texts: "For just as the body is one and has many members, and all the members of the body, though many, are one
body, so it is with Christ. For by one Spirit we are all baptized
into one body—Jews or Greeks, slaves or free—and all were made
to drink of one Spirit" (1 Cor. 12:12-13).

According to Pentecostal theology, the body of Christ is divided
into two distinct groups: those who have been regenerated but

not baptized with the Spirit, and those who have been regenerated and baptized by the Spirit. The New Testament does make distinctions among Christians such as babes in Christ and mature men in Christ, or carnal Christians and spiritual Christians, but never to the point that such distinctions make a division in the body of Christ. The Pentecostal confessions do speak of the one church as the one body of Christ. But do the Pentecostal theologians really know what they have done with the doctrine of the body of Christ by insisting that there is a major distinction among Christians: those who have been justified and are regenerate, and those who in addition to these qualities have been baptized with the Spirit?

This puts Pentecostal theologians between a rock and a hard place. If they claim that they do not functionally or practically divide the body of Christ, then they must greatly minimize the significance of the baptism of the Spirit, for it is no small thing to be incorporated into Christ. If they insist vigorously that the baptism of the Spirit makes a real division among Christians, then they have divided the body of Christ.

If they do not really divide the body of Christ, then what right do they have in making themselves a group of separate denominations built upon a theology which functionally and pragmatically divides the body? Certainly the whole weight of 1 Corinthians 12 is that more important than all gifts is keeping the unity of the body of Christ in the oneness of the Spirit.

In short, we ask our Pentecostal brothers to really get with a mature doctrine of the church and let us know why their doctrine is not a division of the unity of Christ's body.

3. The "body count" of those who have received the second work of grace or second blessing or baptism of the Spirit reveals an interesting datum.

How many Christians in the total history of the Christian church have spoken with tongues or professed this unique experience? When we include the Roman Catholic Church and the various Eastern Orthodox Churches we must say the figure is less than 1 percent.

Yet the claim of the Pentecostal theologians is that the power for living the Christian life and the power for witnessing to the gospel comes from the baptism of the Spirit! Ninety-nine percent of the Christians who are unbaptized by the Spirit have carried the heat of the battle.

If we ask how many Christians have been regenerated, the answer is 100 percent. One cannot be a Christian without being born anew.

If we ask how many Christians have been justified, the answer is 100 percent. One cannot be a Christian without being justified. To this evangelical it is very revealing that Bloch-Hoell had to look and look and look to find a clear statement in Pentecostal literature on justification by faith.

Here is a hard place for Pentecostal theologians. They may wish to raise their percentage by saying many Christians have received the baptism of the Spirit other than Pentecostals. First, it is main-line Pentecostal doctrine that speaking in tongues is *the* sign of the baptism of the Spirit; second, even if speaking in tongues is not the only sign, the sign must be "physical"; third, the sign is so powerful that no one can experience it unwittingly or unknowingly. If these three propositions are true, then we are back to our 1 percent, for that much of a change is not won by affirming that speaking in tongues is not the only sign of the baptism of the Spirit. If that is the case, then the alternative comes down like a ton of bricks: the burden of the survival of Christianity and its missionary propagation rests on the 99 percent of people not baptized with the Holy Spirit. If this is the case, then the Pentecostal doctrine of the necessity of the Spirit's baptism is not so necessary as claimed.

Let us not hurry past this one. There have been great pastors and preachers who have done a monumental work for Jesus Christ who have never experienced in Pentecostalism's terms the baptism of the Spirit. There have been many great missionaries who have lost wife, children, and even their own life or health but yet are unbaptized by the Spirit. Furthermore, there are tens of thousands of faithful, sacrificial Christians dedicated to Christ, to the gospel, and to personal holiness who also have never received the baptism of the Spirit in the terms of Pentecostal theology. I ask simply, directly, honestly and without any venom or hostility: am I to understand that Pentecostal theology makes all of these pastors, missionaries, and Christians second-class citizens in the work of the gospel and in Christian experience?

4. Why is not their interpretation obvious to the great interpreters of the history of the interpretation of Scripture? If a man is going to do real, intense biblical interpretation where are the scientific commentaries written by Pentecostal scholars? In the nineteenth century a number of multivolume commentaries were written by evangelical scholars (Lange's *Commentary;* Ellicott's *Commentary;* the *Speaker's Commentary;* the Jamieson, Fausset and Brown *Commentary*). None of them defend Pentecostal doctrine. Other great German, English, American and French series (Protestant and Roman Catholic) of the twentieth century do not follow Pentecostal theology.

The Pentecostal theologian is caught in another hard place. He not only has to admit that the great bulk of pastors, evangelists, and missionaries of the church have not been baptized by the Holy Spirit but now he has to admit that the vast majority of great commentaries were written by non-Pentecostal theologians.

He might respond that the experiences of Pentecostal people are greater than those of the non-Pentecostal scholars and this makes them "righter" than them all. If the Holy Scripture is the divine authority in the church then it follows that our experiences must conform to Scripture; we cannot torture Scripture to conform to our experiences. If we cannot show by the best interpretation possible that our views are according to the New Testament, what right have we to appeal to experience to support poor exegesis?

No evangelical and no Roman Catholic scholar will claim that God's work can be done without the power of the Holy Spirit. The question is whether the theology of the Pentecostal theologians is true or not.

At this point those who are in conflict with Pentecostal theology are confronted with a real temptation. Those in the traditional churches are likely to say, "Well, we have won the battle of historical theology and biblical interpretation. Let us take our ease."

Hoekema warns us not to take this course.[1] The Pentecostal

1. A. A. Hoekema, *What About Tongue-Speaking?*, chap. 5, "What We Can Learn from the Tongue-Speaking Movement" (Grand Rapids: Eerdmans, 1966).

churches are among the fastest growing churches in the world—at home and abroad. Many of the older denominations are declining in membership, making the contrast even sharper. To win a theological debate or to show that one's interpretation of a doctrine is superior to the interpretation of another Christian does not mean that the winner possesses in his life the power about which he writes. The winner of the academic debate might consequently be the loser in the practicalities of life.

One-grace theology may become Spirit-less orthodoxy. One-grace theology may become grace-less theology. One-grace theology may become a theology without the gifts of the Spirit. One-grace theology may become life-less and routine in its worship services. A theology of power may never become an experience of power. We may claim that we receive all there is of the Spirit in regeneration but show very little of the riches of the Spirit in our concrete Christian experience.

Bibliographical note:

Two books which have gone into the careful interpretation of the texts have provided responsible and reliable evidence to show that the Pentecostal interpretation of the New Testament cannot be sustained: James D. G. Dunn, *Baptism in the Holy Spirit*, no. 15, *Studies in Biblical Theology, Second Series* (London: SCM Press, 1970); and Dale Bruner, *A Theology of the Holy Spirit* (Grand Rapids: Eerdmans, 1970). A more popular analysis is Hoekema's *What About Tongue-Speaking?* referred to earlier in this chapter. Based on my knowledge of the solid exegetical work of Bruner and Dunn, Hollenweger's rejection of their exegesis seems very cavalier, especially in view of the quality of Pentecostal exegesis in general. Cf. *The Pentecostals*, p. 350.

17.

Language and/or tongues?

The issues discussed in this section are so controversial we should again indicate our sources at the start.

We have already referred to Nils Bloch-Hoell, *The Pentecostal Movement*, in the previous section. Its use is occasioned by the international scope of its research and reporting. Dale Bruner's book, *A Theology of the Holy Spirit*, has two important characteristics. First, it is written very clearly with a meticulous outline. It sets out the position of the Pentecostal theologians in one-two-three, apple-pie order. Second, its very extensive documentation shows a comprehensive coverage of the subject matter. In addition I have studied carefully the work of a competent, practicing linguist, William Samarin, who has worked on speaking in tongues in Africa and in America (*Tongues of Men and of Angels*). Samarin includes many transcripts which he has decoded from tapes of people who speak in tongues. These three books cite the Pentecostal writers so profusely that even if one does not read the Pentecostal theologians themselves he will nevertheless gain ample knowledge of their position. An appendix in Bruner's work is composed solely of the reports of the great founders of Pentecostalism of their own experience of speaking in tongues (to Chapter 3). Bruner's bibliography is the most comprehensive that we have encountered.

Again a special word must be said of Hollenweger's *The Pentecostals*. It is a history of the origins of Pentecostalism, a survey of its status in the various countries of the world, and an extensive treatment of its theology. This book may well be the standard encyclopedia of Pentecostalism for some years to come.

Directly to the issue, here are two sections of the New Testament which refer to speaking in tongues: the Book of Acts and 1 Corinthians 12–14. Are they speaking of the same phenomenon? Yes and no. Most Pentecostal theologians believe that speaking in foreign languages is involved in both instances but not necessarily in 1 Corinthians. My own view is that no speaking in foreign tongues (*xenolalia* [Greek *xenos*, foreign, plus *laleō*, to speak]) is taught in 1 Corinthians 12–14 for the following reasons:

In my opinion the speaking in tongues in the Book of Acts was a genuine speaking in a foreign language. The speaking in tongues in the Corinthian letter, on the other hand, was in a non-language, for it required a gift of interpretation equal to the speaking in order to make it understood (1 Cor. 14:13, 27). One theory maintains that the speaking in tongues of Acts 2 was speaking in a common dialect in contrast to the sacred Hebrew. All the scientific lexicographers of the New Testament, however, understand the expression "other tongues" to mean foreign languages.

The reason we separate Acts from 1 Corinthians is that in Acts the fundamental theological issue is as to whether the Holy Spirit is given to certain groups whereas in the Corinthian situation the tongues phenomenon was a highly local matter.

My thesis about Acts is that in every case that men spoke in foreign languages it was a critical situation. All the other places where the gospel was preached (overlooked by Pentecostal theologians and charismatics?) it was received by faith without a speaking in tongues.

My second thesis about Acts is that one cannot create an "Acts theology." The Book of Acts is a book in transit. History—divine history—is on the move! It is the account of how the gospel commenced at Jerusalem and moved step by step until it came to Rome. With the gospel goes the Christian church. At the key junctures in this record of transition men spoke with tongues when they believed the gospel. Therefore these are not normal or usual instances but the unusual. To build a theology of the Holy Spirit primarily on the Book of Acts is contrary to the fundamental Protestant principle of interpretation: *Scripture interprets Scripture*. The great theology of the Holy Spirit is clearest in John's Gospel and Paul's letters. Here is where the great doctors of the church have built their doctrine of the Holy Spirit, and rightly so.

What was special about each of these groups in the Book of Acts?

All are agreed that something which broke out into the open was necessary to announce the arrival of the Holy Spirit on the day of Pentecost. The sound from heaven and the fiery tongues were never repeated. A miraculous speaking in foreign languages was proof to the infant church and to the dwellers and visitors of Jerusalem that something unusual had happened.

The Samaritans (Acts 8:15–17) were a special group in that they did own up to part of the Scripture (the Pentateuch) and did have a temple and priesthood. We learn from John 4 the bitter differences between the Samaritans and the Jews. If the disciples at Jerusalem did not completely control the situation at Samaria, then the infant church would have been divided in its earliest years. It was therefore mandatory that the Spirit be given under the supervision of the Jerusalem church and that the Samaritans receive the same sign as the Jerusalem church—speaking in foreign languages.

The Gentiles (Acts 10:44–47) constituted another key group. God had restricted his revelation to the Hebrews since the call of Abraham in Genesis 12. It had to be demonstrated to their full satisfaction that the Gentiles could truly believe and did truly receive the same Holy Spirit the Jews had received at Pentecost. Speaking in foreign languages was adequate to establish both points.

The disciples of John the Baptist formed another special group (Acts 19:5–6). The kingdom of God was announced by John the Baptist. What was the status of his baptism as related to Christian baptism? What was the status of those who believed him with reference to the Messiah? The answer is clear in Acts 19. They did not receive the Holy Spirit because, as the context shows, they did not believe in Christ. Only when they believed in Christ were they given the gift of the Spirit.

In no manner does the non-language of the church at Corinth carry the theological weight that speaking in languages does in the Book of Acts. This is the reason for my belief that there is every theological reason to separate 1 Corinthians from the Book of Acts.

Further, I believe that the tongues of Corinth were a non-language or gibberish. Nothing prejudicial is meant by using the word *gibberish*. I am indicating simply that these are not known languages but a special kind of devotional and inspirational language.

First, I believe that a careful study of 1 Corinthians 14 warrants our calling these tongues non-languages.

Second, I believe the studies of contemporary linguists show that these tongues were non-languages.

However, it is claimed by Pentecostals that they can authenticate many instances of Pentecostals speaking in foreign languages. Bloch-Hoell (pp. 142ff.) indicates four different kinds of speaking in tongues: (i) inarticulate sounds or utterings; (ii) articulate sounds or pseudo-language; (iii) articulate and combined language-like sounds; and (iv) genuine foreign languages—xenolalia.

It is the last of these with which we are concerned. Bloch-Hoell gives some professed examples, citing among others a Pentecostal leader named Barratt who claimed he spoke in eight foreign languages one night. Samarin also discusses this phenomenon and shows linguistically how this could happen. To date there are no sufficient controls on these foreign language incidents to warrant their acceptance. In that speaking in tongues claimed by sects, cults, and non-Christian religions it may be a human possibility capable of a natural explanation. To Pentecostals who believe that speaking in actual foreign languages occurs in their groups we affirm two things: (1) That may well be, but as yet the phenomenon has not been carefully observed by professional linguists so that there can be competent verification of it. (2) If we do not understand that the New Testament teaches this phenomenon as one Christians should, or must, experience, then we are faced with a decision for the New Testament or for the experiences of the Pentecostals. We therefore stay with the New Testament, for we know that is the revelation of God.

Obviously some sort of unusual phenomenon took place in the Corinthian church. According to 1 Corinthians 12–14, and according to the witness of contemporary charismatics or neo-Pentecostals, this speaking in tongues is for worship, edification, and personal devotions. This is apparently the legitimate and proper use of tongues in the Christian fellowship. By the same token it further justifies my conviction that the Book of Acts records something very different from what took place at Corinth.

One more item needs comment. Why should the church at Corinth be singled out and made normative for all Christians? If the Pentecostal doctrine of baptism with the Spirit manifest in speaking in tongues or some other equally manifest sign is so absolutely cardinal to the life of the church, why does not Paul spell it out in great detail as he does the other great motifs of his theology? Why is there no mention of the Pentecostal phenomenon or at least speaking in tongues in his other letters? It seems odd to an evangelical who is neither a Pentecostal nor a neo-Pentecostal that so much Pentecostal theology is built upon the Book of Acts, which reflects the church in a highly transitional period of its life, and upon the correspondence with the Corinthian church, which was Paul's most eccentric church. The contrast with the great theological passages in Romans, Galatians, Ephesians, Colossians, Hebrews and 1 John is too sharp.

Again we are back to the great Reformation motto: Scripture interprets Scripture. All special pleading from Acts and 1 Corinthians has not come to terms with this motto. The Pentecostal theologians must face a hard decision: which is really the most powerful factor in their thinking, their own experiences or the authority of the New Testament over all man's experiences? If they insist that their experiences are more enlightening about the meaning of the New Testament than the most solid exposition possible then they have broken with the universal Christian principle of authority: the authority of Holy Scripture over all that men claim or experience.

Appendix

For those who have never seen a transcript of the phenomenon of speaking in tongues we append a partial one from William J. Samarin's book, *Tongues of Men and Angels*.[1] Samarin has a number of such transcripts and we commend his book to those who wish to examine this phenomenon more thoroughly from a linguistic standpoint. The speaker is a Rev. D'Esprit [French for "Reverend Mr. Spirit"] whom Samarin uses as his model speaker in tongues:

1. kupóy shăndré fĭlé sundrukumă shăndré lása hóya tăkí. 2. fozhŏn shĕtírĕloso kumó shăndré palasó shăntré kamóyĕntri. 3. sózhăndri kága sómbo póyĕntrĕ lapatsómbo kóyshăntrala só. 4. fĭlă săndrúzhăntrăkămălă sĭndrí patató săntrăkú zhăndré. 5. kílă só zhăndrámăndrăfulu sú shăntrí lĭmétăki. 6. mozăndro folĕsĭtĕrá sumprúturut fulĭsĭntráyindri kămpătăkă fulăsó. 7. kézhăndri tarasómbo kayandré. 8. fíli sĭndrí tărotú săntrăkădĭ shin drĭpĭti píli săntró. 9. nésăntro fĭlé săntrí káyăntroposhănträ méri kílisu. 10. fíli sĭndrí káyĕntro móshĕntrĕ pĕlĕsŏndo. 11. shĭndrí katári pilí sĭndrí kízhăn drúpu lăsúnt. 12. kambóyăntre filasín zhíndra mú. 13. fálasun drúshăntă káli síntratirăl súmpăke. 14. fĭlă sózhăn drómă tărípili síndri kí. 15. kúzhăntray pilisín zhăndrumăndára fĭlĭsĭntrú. 16. sazhándĕrĕ kélă sĭntrú pătăsámbo kóyăntay. 17. sizhăndrepí tărú shăntrăkó. 18.

1. *Tongues of Men and Angels* by William J. Samarin (Copyright © 1972 by William J. Samarin). Used by permission.

118

Bibliographical note:

William J. Samarin's *Tongues of Men and Angels* is a remarkable
contribution to the subject from a linguistic standpoint. He shows by
the use of several transcripts from tapes that what is said does not
have the structure of a language; hence our term, non-language.
For a thorough exegesis of the Acts passages showing that the Pentecostal exegesis does not make its case, see Dale Bruner, *A Theology
of the Holy Spirit*. James D. G. Dunn's *Baptism in the Spirit* is a
careful work centering on the conversion and initiation experience.
Although it is essentially a study in biblical theology it does interact
with the opinions of the Roman Catholic, Reformed, and Lutheran
views, and the views of the Pentecostals. Hollenweger notes that
Pentecostal theology is built mainly on Luke's writings in the Gospel
of Luke and the Book of Acts, and that traditional theology is built
more on Paul's writings. Then he makes the odd decision that he
opts for Luke over against Paul (*The Pentecostals*, pp. 341, 350.)
This is odd for two reasons: (1) The rule of Protestant biblical interpretation that Scripture interprets Scripture is broken if an interpreter pits Luke against Paul or Paul against Luke. Granted, each
writer of the New Testament has his perspective that is not to be
artlessly reduced to some other writer's perspective; but to pit Luke
against Paul as Hollenweger does is the end of the unity of Scripture
and the end of the golden rule of Protestant theology that Scripture
interprets Scripture. Has the Pentecostal movement come anywhere
near maturity in Biblical interpretation? (2) Paul is considered *the*
theologian of the church with his thirteen epistles. How odd, then,
to choose Luke over Paul! Is this not a case of a thesis highly select-
ing its evidence in order to survive? Certainly Paul does not lay it
down line upon line that one must be baptized with the Spirit and
speak in tongues to do effective evangelistic work or successfully live
the Christian life. If the Pentecostal theologians choose Luke over
Paul they are digging a theological and exegetical hole which they
will fall into and which they may find most embarrassing to have to
crawl out of.

18.

Charismatics and neo-Pentecostals

Neo-Pentecostalism is the term used to describe the charismatic movement in the Protestant and Roman Catholic churches. Less doctrinaire than Pentecostalism per se, it operates in a lower or "quieter" key and stresses other gifts than tongues as equally important. Some neo-Pentecostals are more interested in healing (broadly understood so as to include mental health) than in tongues.

This movement is difficult to assess. Something has caused it to come into being. Understanding something that is taking place *in medias res*—in our midst—carries a problem of perspective. Further, when a person is not a member of the in-group of a movement he misses many of the dynamics of the movement; if one has not had a charismatic experience, the experience is opaque to him. I miss on both counts. But when it's his turn in the batting order, the player has to go to bat, and I'll take mine now.

There are different theories why the neo-Pentecostal movement has emerged. We shall attempt to assess the movement by looking at the theories.

1. It is a movement inspired by the Holy Spirit himself. He has seen fit to call the church back to himself, his power, and his ministries. The church without his gifts is a weaker, poorer church.

This theory is stated in the *Report of the Special Committee on the work of the Holy Spirit* of The United Presbyterian Church in the United States of America (Philadelphia, 1970). This report, jammed with important material, judicious and preeminently fair, contains the following comment on page 3:

119

It is very possible that the Holy Spirit is preparing a renewal of the Church in our time that may come in surprising ways and through unexpected channels. We are therefore conscious that, in addressing ourselves to the question of glossolalia and other unusual manifestations, we are dealing with only one small segment of a vast theme that has enormous potential for the Church.

2. It could be that the neo-Pentecostal movement is a reaction to certain elements in the contemporary church. There are a number of possibilities here.

First, there was a charismatic movement in the major denominations before the youth rebellion of our times broke out. Either the charismatics were sensitive to pressures before the youth were, or else the stimulus came from something in the church. One possibility is that a modern denomination is so highly structured and organized that a pastor feels this stifling and controlling rather than helpful. Or perhaps the theological diversity in our denominations is so great that it is frustrating. Or again, the emphasis on success in terms of numbers, increased budgets, and successful programs could irritate those more interested in the divine way of reckoning success.

Second, the Christian layman or pastor may feel that the church is too much a part of the Establishment, or system. In the search for a truly humanitarian ethic that respects persons in the maximum degree a church may seem cold and officious.

What can Christians do when they feel that their denomination has become a leviathan or that its theological diversity is impossible to live with? They may split and go independent, and some have done this. Or, ignoring the leviathan, they can turn completely inward and live their Christian lives totally within their own local church. Or they can turn to the charismatic movement, where a fresh breathing of the Spirit seems to be taking place. In this movement Christians may find a new openness for the Spirit, a real regard for persons as persons, and a real appreciation for a life of true piety.

3. If the earlier charismatic movement—sporadically in evidence in the fifties—was caused by a restlessness within the institutional church, then the Jesus People are part of the social unrest of our times.

There is no question that we are going through a cultural revolution. It was anticipated by the prophets of the doom of Western culture in the nineteenth and early twentieth centuries (Nietzsche, Spengler, and others). Two world wars and a depression apparently staved off the event. When it did come, it came as a youth rebellion against the system or the establishment.

One of the most successful efforts to describe this new youth mentality was *It's Happening: A Portrait of the Youth Scene Today,* by J. L. Simmons and Barry Winograd.[1] James Michener has attempted to do the same thing in fiction by giving a lengthy biographical sketch of his major characters in his novel *The Drifters.*[2]

Any major shift in culture has its religious counterparts. A shift in youth culture will be reflected in a shift in our religious young people. A number of stirrings have manifested themselves among the young people in the late part of the 1960s and the early part of the 1970s, ranging from the very proper Campus Crusade to the charismatic Jesus People to the unexpected Evangelical Radicals.

Basic social unrest becomes also unrest with the church. If a person has a deep spiritual concern he may cop out from the system or from the church but not from Christian faith. Such a person who wants a non-system church may find what he wants in neo-Pentecostalism.

It is harder to analyze the Roman Catholic version of neo-Pentecostalism, as this apparently involves a great number of followers well beyond their twenties. The number of Roman Catholic neo-Pentecostals is estimated between 60,000 and 100,000. The last Pentecostal Catholic conference at Notre Dame registered 11,000 attendants.[3] There must be pressures both within and without the Roman Catholic Church to create a movement of this dimension.

I am not attempting to engage in a reductionist's argument. All of us are subject to all sorts of pressures. Genuine convictions and pressures need not be posed as conflicting or as antithetical.

1. Santa Barbara: Marc-Laird Publications, 1966.
2. Greenwich, Conn.: Fawcett, Great Books, 1971.
3. Cf. Richard J. Mouw, "Catholic Pentecostalism Today," and a parallel article by Marlin Van Elderen, "Explo '72 and Campus Crusade," both in *The Reformed Journal,* 22:8ff., July-August 1972.

There is no conclusive evidence as yet that the neo-Pentecostal movement uniformly attracts a certain psychological type, although some observations are to be taken seriously (e.g., that some speakers in tongues are of a dependent nature and are sustained only through close identification with Pentecostal leadership and a Pentecostal fellowship). The same is true in attempting to explain the phenomenon by showing neo-Pentecostals as coming from a certain typical social background.

The New Testament teaches that some Christians may do the work of God in a manner that other Christians reject. Christians ought then to be careful before they reject something as unchristian on the grounds that it does not fit into their conception of how God is working in the world.

The disciples prevented a man from casting out demons, for though he did it in the name of Christ he was not part of the apostolic company. Our Lord's reply was: "Do not forbid him; for he that is not against you is for you" (Luke 9:49–50, RSV).

When Paul was in prison at Philippi some men preached in the streets as Paul had preached to make more trouble for him. Paul's response was: "Only that in every way, whether in pretense or in truth, Christ is proclaimed; and in that I rejoice" (Phil. 1:18, RSV).

As much as neo-Pentecostalism and the charismatic movement may gall more traditional churchmen, these injunctions of the New Testament must be remembered and carefully considered before any condemnation is pronounced.

Having been told to judge spirits, however, I feel the need to register a *caveat* (Latin: "let him be aware"):

1. *A caveat of doctrine.* Paul says that no man claiming to speak from the impulse of the Spirit can say that Jesus is accursed (1 Cor. 12:1–3). This would be contrary to the teaching of the New Testament that Jesus is Lord. In the same way, nothing that the neo-Pentecostals claim that goes contrary to the theology of the New Testament can be of the Holy Spirit. If the Jesus People develop a "Jesusology" that is a repudiation of the doctrine of the Trinity then that Jesusology is not of the Holy Spirit.

2. *A caveat for unity.* The emphasis on the unity of spiritual gifts in 1 Corinthians 12 is so great it must mean that the exercise of gifts in the Corinthian church was divisive. Certainly that has

been one of the tender spots of the charismatic movement. How can a man possess a gift in humility? How can a group of charismatics meet within a church fellowship and not become a little church? Paul is emphatic. There is one Spirit and one only behind all the rich diversity of spiritual gifts. Even though there is a wonderful diversity of members in the body of Christ, it is one body. To the degree that neo-Pentecostalism becomes an entity in itself it is contrary to the New Testament teaching of gifts and of the one body of Christ. To the degree that charismatic individuals divide the body of Christ they are schismatics. No person can claim something is of the Spirit if it does that which is contrary to the Spirit, namely, if in small or in large it divides the body of Christ.

3. *A caveat about authority.* It is a trait of any Christian who has had a remarkable experience to move from his experience to the interpretation of the New Testament. This is contrary to the way the church has traditionally regarded the authority of the New Testament. It is the New Testament which screens experience. The New Testament does not discuss all possible valid experiences. It does discuss those lines which no experience can cross and still be called Christian.

It is an obvious and serious temptation of charismatics to move from their experiences to the interpretation of the New Testament. It is the conviction of the evangelical grounded in biblical theology and historical theology that the New Testament must assess experience rather than experience pushing the New Testament around so that it agrees with experience.

Bibliographical note:

Whether the neo-Pentecostals are a definite psychological type or are products of certain sociological situations is carefully analyzed and assessed by Samarin in *Tongues of Men and Angels,* chap. 2, "Explained Psychologically." Much valuable information is also contained in the Presbyterian Report cited in the text. A. A. Hoekema also discusses the neo-Pentecostals in *What About Tongue-Speaking?* In addition to the report in the *Reformed Journal* there is one in the British publication *TSF Bulletin:* Greg S. Forster, "The Third Arm: Pentecostal Christianity," 63:5–9, Summer 1972. The article is substantially documented and was due to be continued in a future issue.

19.

The Spirit
and goody-goody Christians

Back in the neolithic period of American education when my
generation went to school it was continuously drilled into our
little minds that we were to be people of character. But for all
the dinning and drilling not too much got through. We still pep-
pered our young contemporaries with spit-wads. We still forged
our excuses for being absent. We still smoked cigarettes behind
garages or in alleys or in a copse of woods.

Sunday school wasn't much different. We teased our teachers
until they went bananas and gave up the class. We kept out our
collection money and spent it on movies Sunday afternoon. At
school we told off-color jokes along with the other kids. During
church we drew cartoons on the visitors' cards or the collection
envelopes or the church bulletin.

So, what makes a person good or want to be good? When does
careless, even irresponsible behavior give way to conduct based
on character? When do we want to do something out of the goodness of our hearts instead of by threat (or in the language of
ethics, by sanctions)?

It is the age-old problem of motivation. In my opinion the
theory of motivation that has characterized the history of ethics
is that of Plato. Plato taught that if we really knew the good we
would always do good and not evil. The question is: when do I
really know the good? Motivation from the Greek and Roman
educational systems has centered in pain and punishment. From
the time of the Greeks until early in the twentieth century school
children have been beaten and pounded. Today psychologists like

B. F. Skinner would reverse the process and motivate children by rewards (operant conditioning).

In the Christian faith we appear to motivate Christians to be "goody-goody" Christians, to use the vernacular. Christians are not especially different from the rest of humanity, and motivation is as much a problem among them as it is in our society and school system. How do we get Christians on the move?

There are several facets to the Christian doctrine of motivation in Christian ethics. Romans 6 is a magnificent treatise on Christian motivation. We who are Christ's in baptism have been crucified to our old life of sin and our old sinful nature and we are made alive to God and righteousness through sharing Christ's resurrection. The present discussion, however, will be limited to one facet of Christian motivation, namely, the motivation which comes from the Holy Spirit.

The place of beginning is Romans 5:5. The context is justification by faith. One of the great blessings of justification by faith is that God has sent the Holy Spirit into the heart of the believer. The Holy Spirit in turn sheds the love of God abroad in the heart of the believer. The Spirit is there in the power of love to motivate Christians to be good, that is, to do the will of God in moral and ethical decisions.

One of the common terms in psychological jargon is "to internalize." In more prosaic language this means to make something our own. A child might be told a million times to be neat. When he goes off to college and keeps his room neat he has internalized the housekeeping standards of his parents. One of the most difficult of all human endeavors is to have our children internalize moral standards. It is the New Testament teaching that the Holy Spirit helps the Christian internalize the ethical teachings of the New Testament—not that this is easy! James 4:5 sets forth an internal struggle in the Christian. The Holy Spirit contests the human spirit which is pulled in a wayward direction. Christians too live in a gravitational field of sin. But the Holy Spirit is there to combat the pull of the gravity of sin. While the flesh-bound nature of man pulls in the wrong direction the Holy Spirit is present attempting—even more, striving—to internalize moral standards in the believer.

Another very rich chapter on the work of the Spirit in internalizing Christian morality is 2 Corinthians 3. Paul says that the morality of the New Covenant is written on the heart of the Christian by the Holy Spirit. Christian morality is not keeping the law which is an external code written on lifeless stone. This is, again, in our language, the internalization of morality. If morality is internalized in a person, by the very definition of internalization that person will live out the Christian ethic. The basic problem of motivation is settled.

Although the Holy Spirit solves the problem of internalizing, in Christian ethical theory, we must be careful not to overstate our case. The Christian ought not to claim too much. Luther knew of the frailty of Christians on this earth and that they are justified but not glorified. He expressed this frailty in two of his most famous sayings: "Sin bravely," and, Christians are "at the same time justified and yet sinners." "Sin bravely" means that the Christian ought not be disheartened by the fact that he sins. Justification is not perfection nor glorification. Christians fight the world, the flesh, and devil *all the days of their lives!* There is no let-up in this battle. There is no point at which we crest a summit and may relax our watch. It stands to reason we shall lose some skirmishes—yes, even battles—to the world or the flesh or the devil. To "sin bravely" means that when that happens the Christian does not throw in the sponge claiming all is lost or all is impossible. To the contrary, he bravely gets up like a veteran soldier and continues to push the battle. He knows that God knows our frailty, our weakness, and that we are but flesh. He knows that God knows the power of evil in this world. He knows of God's infinite provisions of grace for forgiveness and restoration through the cross of Jesus Christ. Having lost a skirmish or a battle, the Christian does not lay down shield and sword but confesses his sin, enjoys the blessing of forgiveness and restoration, and carries on his combat.

The other phrase expresses the paradoxical nature of Christian experience that Christians of a certain stripe always try to eliminate. These are the perfectionist Christians who wish to destroy the paradoxical nature of Christian experience and see man only as justified. Luther knew better both from his study of Scripture and his personal experience. Salvation in this life is not perfection, nor sinlessness, nor glorification. Its paradoxical character which allows Christians to be at the same time saints and sinners cannot and must not be denied.

Be that as it may, the Spirit still is a plus value that the Christian has in his ethical struggles. From the Spirit comes motivation and power foreign to a purely philosophical or humanistic ethic. Not all Christians claim this resource or enjoy its benefits, of course. But it is there according to the word of divine revelation and, being there, it gives Christian ethics a unique dimension.

This unique dimension exists potentially in Judaism through the Old Testament doctrine of the Holy Spirit. Although the Spirit is mentioned in the Qu'ran, the references are of such nature as to indicate that while Mohammed had heard of the doctrine of the Spirit from Jews and/or Christians, he did not understand the theology of the Spirit.

Bibliographical note:

Most of the books on the theology of the Holy Spirit contain some
materials on the power of the Holy Spirit in Christian living. However, cf. also Leon Morris, *Spirit of the Living God* (London: Inter-
Varsity Press, 1960). Fredrick Wisløff, *I Believe in the Holy Spirit*.
In German there is the extensive work of Kurt Stalder, *Das Werk
des Geistes in der Heiligung bei Paulus* (Zürich: EVZ Verlag, 1962).
C. G. Mylrea, *The Holy Spirit in the Qu'ran and Bible* (London: The
Christian Literature Society for India, 1910) is an examination of
all the references to the Spirit in the Qu'ran showing Mohammed's
lack of understanding of the doctrine of the Spirit.

20.

Does the Spirit have a tongue?

The Day of Pentecost has been called "the Christmas of the Holy Spirit." Just as there was the advent of the second person of the Trinity into the world at Christmas, there was the advent of the third person at Pentecost. Our Lord's promise that another Counselor would come (John 14:16) means that he was the first. In John 14:18 our Lord further said that he would not leave his disciples orphans—as the Greek text has it and not "desolate" as the RSV translates it. Pentecost is, then, the advent or coming of the Holy Spirit as the permanent Counselor of the church and as the One who indwells every believer.

Our Lord came in a "worldly" fashion, that is, he was born a man, amongst men, and lived as a man. It is the earthly life of the Incarnate Christ which gives concreteness and hence richness and tangibility to such abstractions as love, grace, pity, and forgiveness. The Spirit too must make a worldly appearance so that we may know he has come and is here. Further, that part of the mystery of his being "spirit" will be relieved as he breaks out into the open. This he did with signs of his coming such as a sound from heaven coming and filling the house, tongues of fire resting on each apostle, and then the speaking in other tongues.

Why is the tongue the supreme sign of the coming of the Spirit as represented in the tongues of fire and then the speaking in tongues? Why should the One without a body be signified by the bodily part of the tongue?

To begin with, the word *tongue* means language as in our expression *mother tongue*. So the questions move on to another plane. Why should speaking a language be so closely associated with the Holy Spirit? Or, why should the phenomenon of speech be so closely associated with the Holy Spirit?

The answer must be that there is something theological or spiritual or ontological (i.e., referring to reality) about speech. The question is: if so, what is it?

At the outset we can rid our minds of speech as purely and only a signaling or encoding device. Speech is not a simple process of taking a thought in one's head, speaking it by means of one's vocal cords, transmitting it through the ears of the hearer, and then having the meaning registered in the mind of the others. It is not an elaborate organic (in contrast to an electrical or electronic system) telegraphing system. It is much deeper than that.

One of the cues that speech is buried deeply within the self is that when people approach death they are prone to relapse into their mother language if they have migrated from their homeland and have had to learn a second language. When, for instance, a European who has migrated to America in his final days reaches the border between waking and coma where consciousness and unconsciousness become difficult to define, he may well lapse into his mother-tongue. That language is still residing in the "archaic self" and at the time of the transition from time to eternity rises again to the surface.

Another clue to the way in which the self and speech are so intimately associated is again illustrated by a person who knows two languages. If asked which language will best express his thoughts, he will usually say he can do it best in his mother-language. However, modern linguists will say that there is no such thing as a superior language as Greek and then Latin were once thought to be. All languages can eventually say what they want to say. The conviction that one's mother tongue is the best vehicle for expressing oneself is not a commentary on the superiority of that language but rather demonstrates the depth to which the self and its mother language are identified.

Another clue to the profound character of speech can be found among missionaries. If speech were purely for signs of communication and an easy method of passing on information then a poor speaker would be like a poor baseball player. We would consider that he played a poor ball game but he does not spiritually distress us. In sharp contrast, how well a given missionary knows the tribal or national language of the people he is serving is a matter of serious concern. His effectiveness as a missionary and his very status may eventually be assessed by his mastery or lack of mastery of the local language. Language command is a touchy and emotional subject among missionaries. The status of one's language skill is more than the status of a skill; it reflects the profound existential nature of speech.

Another clue that language is "existential" is our use of speech not only to express ideas but emotions and attitudes. We convey by language what is deepest in us, namely, our feelings. Emotional disorders may crop up in speech. At the most innocent level are Freudian slips. A Freudian slip in our language is the term to describe what happens when we think one thing and intend to say another but say the thing we think. Rodney, a dumb and naive knight in the comic strip "The Wizard of Id," may say "There goes the fink," instead of "There goes the king." A deeper pathology is stuttering and stammering. Because a person who stutters can usually sing without trouble, the disorder is not thought to be neurological. There are many theories concerning the cause for stuttering. One of the more recent is that the child who stutters has had a very demanding parent. The child feels that it must speak perfectly to please the parent but overcompensates and ends up in stuttering.

Muslims certainly regard Arabic as having "existential" qualities. To them the revelation given to Mohammed and recorded in the Qu'ran can only truly be understood in the Arabic. All translations are feeble efforts in reproducing the thought of the Qu'ran. The Arabic script of the Qu'ran, written out in a very elaborate form, has an additional "existential" character. (There are several such elaborate Arabic scripts as the Kufic, Naskhi, Thuluth, and Tughra). The Muslim call to prayer, the prayers in the mosque, and the reading of the Qu'ran all existentially "grab" the devout Muslim. None of this could be unless language had this existential dimension which is more than simple communication.

There is such a thing as a philosophy of language, that is, the conviction that language has an ontological (referring to reality) status. Grammarians of a language may write a book on the syntax of the language. Linguists study the phenomenon of speech as such. Not one language but all languages are their concern. This is not ontological. A philosopher of language may believe that speech is ontological because its essence is not disclosed by the grammarian nor by the linguist. Such different scholars as Dilthey, Heidegger, and recently Dewart come to mind here. There is also in theology a school stemming from Heidegger which believes that language is itself the clue to man and reality: the New Hermeneutic.

A person who believes language is ontological believes that the grammarian and the linguist stop at what has been called the semantic view of language (i.e., language as primarily signs). This must move on to the syntactical view of language (i.e., language is the means of sharing and disclosing reality). If speech is profoundly a part of the self it cannot also be other than the mirror of the self. The speech of a righteous man will ultimately let the righteousness hidden in his self shine out just as the speech of a wicked man will eventually unmask his wickedness.

Scripture itself assigns great seriousness to speech when it says that what we confess (before God in awful solemnity) saves us (Rom. 9:9–10) and what we say in unbelief and blasphemy damns us (Matt. 12:37).

If speech is spiritual, existential, and ontological we can then get our first glimmer why the tongue is the sign of the Spirit. If God's Spirit is the immediate touch of God on the creature, and if speech is the primary means of the disclosure of the self, then there is no wonder that the tongue is the symbol of the Spirit. John tells us that it is a man's language which betrays or reveals what spirit or Spirit is prompting him (1 John 4:1–3). Paul says that the human tongue can confess that Jesus is Lord only under the prompting of the Holy Spirit (1 Cor. 12:3).

Not all human speaking is existential or personal or spiritual or ontological; all these terms are approximations or synonyms of one underlying idea. Social formalities like "How are you?" or "Glad to see you," or "It is a nice day, isn't it?" are not to be taken seriously. Propositions in mathematics and logic are to be viewed as pure abstractions and devoid of emotional content—unless brought into a context where some human decision lies in the application of the proposition. Ordinarily we take speech seriously in the most serious part of human experience and knowledge. The taking of wedding vows or an oath in a court of law are considered very serious speaking. We furthermore believe that when a man speaks of his philosophy or his religion he is speaking with utmost seriousness.

Scripture considers speech directed to God the most important speech that man can engage in. Hence confession, adoration, praise, and decision are central in biblical religion and worship. If speech comes to its most serious manifestation in speech to God then we get another insight as to why speech can be so intimately associated with the Holy Spirit.

It is the philosopher Heidegger who has worked out in most detail what kind of speech is real, authentic speech and what kind is superficial and inauthentic. Real talk is *Reden* (from the German verb *reden*, to speak); superficial talk is *Gerede*—gossip. In gossip I pull myself and my responsibility out of my language! I am talking about "other people" and not about myself.

Real, authentic writing (*Schreiben*) degenerates into scribbling (*Geschriebe*) when I do not put myself into my writing. I write again about other people and not about myself. Real speech is prompted by the Holy Spirit (if one is talking about spiritual matters) as is real writing; but gossip and scribbling are not only prompted by man's sinnerhood but are a serious expression of sin as man divorces his true self from his speaking and writing.

If speech is existential in this broad sense then we must take a second look at what happened at Pentecost. Seen from this perspective, Pentecost was more than a miracle of linguistics. It must be seen as a profoundly spiritual, existential, and theological event. Pentecost, as theologians have said, was the reversal of Babel. The confusion of man's language was a way of combatting man's willful efforts to defy God. The most radical difference among men is not that of culture or physique but of language. Augustine knew this centuries ago when he wrote:

> For if two men, each ignorant of the other's language, meet, and are not compelled to pass, but, on the contrary, to remain in company, dumb animals, though of different species, would more easily hold intercourse than they, human beings though they be.

For their common nature is no help to friendliness when they are prevented by diversity of language from conveying their sentiments to one another; so that a man would more readily hold intercourse with his dog than with a foreigner (*City of God*, xix/7).

Between Babel and Pentecost were the incarnation, death, and resurrection of Christ. The New Testament identifies this series of events with the redemption or reconciliation of the world. God's act of reconciliation in Christ must be personally appropriated, however: "We beseech you on behalf of Christ, be reconciled to God" (2 Cor. 5:20). Pentecost was the day when the apostles of Christ made their first public pronouncement of God's redemptive work in Christ, and offered its benefits to the hearers who would receive it by repentance and faith.

One of the facets of this great day was, then, the reversal of Pentecost. Whether the miracle was something which happened to the speaker or occurred in the ear of the hearer does not alter this assertion one way or the other. The important point is that this miracle took place within the context of the ongoing history of redemption and on one of its most critical days of that entire history.

Can we stop here? If the Spirit creates the beautiful in some sense there is beauty in the Spirit. If the Spirit can give the gift of languages there is then something about speech in the Spirit. Or phrased another way, there must be an intimate relationship between speech and the Holy Spirit. But this thought will have its proper significance only if the preceding exposition is kept in mind, namely, that speech not only conveys information but has an existential, spiritual, interpretative, and emotional depth.

Seen in this perspective, it now becomes clearer why the inspiration of the biblical writers and the production of an inspired Scripture is ascribed to the Holy Spirit. Writing is an extension of speaking, for linguists uniformly affirm that speech is prior to and deeper than writing. If the Holy Spirit is a Spirit of language he is then also a Spirit of language in written form. The inspiration of Scripture is to be seen not as purely the action of the power of the Spirit and the gifts of the Spirit, but also as the product of One who in ways unknown to us is profoundly connected with the human activity of speaking and writing.

Added to this is the association of the Spirit with the hearing of the Word. Speech involves the hearer as much as the speaker, and hearing is almost as complicated a neurological and mental activity as speaking. Again it is the Spirit that enables us to experience illumination of the Word of God. It is the Spirit that enables our ears to hear revelation as revelation. The Spirit not only loosens the tongue but he opens the ear.

Again we cannot say too much. Anthropologists and linguists have suggested many theories of the origin of speech. To date the verification of any such theories appears impossible. It is a real temptation at this time to claim that the Holy Spirit solves the riddle of man's ability to speak. That is as much a "faith claim" as the other linguistic theories are "hypotheses." However, if we restrain from affirming that we can prove that speech is the gift of the Spirit to man, we need not be restrained in the other direction. There is a real connection between the Holy Spirit and speech and it is this real connection which lies behind the phenomena of the day of Pentecost. But seeing that beauty and speech are somehow "imbedded" in the Holy Spirit we give the Spirit flesh and blood, that is, more concrete reality, or are more able to envision him as a person in contrast to the idea of Spirit as being pure power, pure presence, and pure immanence.

Bibliographical note:

For the insight into speech and the Holy Spirit I am indebted to Abraham Kuyper, *The Work of the Spirit*, chap. 18, "The Miracle of Tongues." For Jewish opinions about speech as a gift to man at Creation and the relationship of the Spirit to the inspired speech of the prophets, see J. Massingberg Ford, "Towards a Theology of 'Speaking in Tongues,'" *Theological Studies*, 32:2–29, March 1971. For the details of the New Testament use of the word *tongues* see Johannes Behm, "*glossa*," *Theological Dictionary of the New Testament*, 1:719–726.

21.

Prayer as seen from the launch pad

Is prayer truly petitionary (asking and receiving) or is it part of personal renewal and regrouping of one's resources? Does God answer prayer in some real, "external" manner, or is prayer only meditation about God and communion with him? If a theologian omits the Holy Spirit in this discussion he cannot find the right answer. Prayer is generally agreed to originate with man and terminate with God. But how does it get off the launch pad with man? Therein lies the answer to the real nature of prayer: if it involves the Holy Spirit it must be petitionary.

Paul tells us that we do not know what to pray for, that is, what we want God to do (Rom. 8:26). This Paul attributes to our weakness. "Weakness" in this passage speaks of the moral and spiritual weakness of all men as sinners. A spiritually weak person (again, that which all sinners are, including Christians) in this sense cannot perceive what is the will of God for which he should pray. He neither sees the mind of God clearly enough nor does he know the factors in the world well enough to know how to pray the right petition.

Every missile launched into space is under constant watch from the mission control center and its trajectory continuously checked. When there is a fractional deviation which may in the great distances traveled add up to tens of thousands of miles, that deviation is corrected. So it is with our prayers. Prayer is something human beings launch! God can no more do our praying for us than he can exercise faith for us. Our dilemma is that we cannot launch our prayers true to the divine trajectory, yet we

138

must pray! Because we pray "off course," even in contradiction to the intention of God, God must use a correctional device. It is the Holy Spirit who functions as the Divine Corrector. The Spirit, knowing the mind of God, knows the intentions of God. The Spirit, knowing our hearts, knows what we truly want and need. Knowing the origin of prayer, the human heart, and the terminus of prayer, the divine Majesty, he corrects the prayer so that it zooms into correct focus.

What we can do correctly is to pray in good faith—for James (4:3) indicates that we can pray in bad faith. When we do pray in good faith, however amiss of the divine intention, the Spirit refashions those prayers with "sighs too deep for words" so that when they reach the ear of the Father they are "according to the will of God" (Rom. 8:27).

Jude implores us to pray in the Holy Spirit (Jude 20). What can this possibly mean but to pray "ecstatically"? The Greek word means "to stand outside [of oneself]" and is similar to our expression "he is beside himself." To be ecstatic or to be beside oneself means to be in a state out of the ordinary.

The athlete is ecstatic when he puts forth an effort far beyond what is necessary in daily life, for example, when he jumps seven feet high or runs a mile in under four minutes. The entertainer is ecstatic when he does something with a class or polish or finesse or talent one does not find in the common herd.

To pray in the Holy Spirit is then to perform like the athlete or entertainer to get oneself out of the ordinary, to break with the humdrum level of talking, interacting, and participating. Conversation with heaven must be ecstatic conversation. It is not so much an ecstasy of an unusual psychological state, but of seriousness of intention, of intensity of purpose, and a feeling of awe before the One to whom we pray. It may be the silent praying of a Hannah or the audible prayer of a David, distraught upon his bed during the night finding relief only as he tries literally to lift his voice to God.

To pray in the Spirit means to be empowered in our prayers by the Spirit. We and we alone can pray, but we can be empowered in our prayers. The human side of praying in the Spirit is to pray with an intensity that is spiritually exhausting. When

Jesus healed he felt the depletion of his spiritual powers (Mark 5:30). It is a common confession of all charismatics that praying, and, especially, praying for the sick, is physically exhausting.

From the divine side this kind of prayer can be done only in the Holy Spirit. Only he can help us pray that prayer which is exhausting. Gethsemane is the pattern for this kind of prayer. That agony was possible only "in the Spirit." If we would pray like our Lord in Gethsemane we must pray in the Spirit.

To pray in the Spirit means to be in immediate communion with God. We need no means of transmission like telephone lines or electromagnetic waves as in television broadcasting. The line of communication from the heart of the believer to the Throne of Grace (Heb. 4:16) is the Holy Spirit. The theological dust tossed into the air by Bishop Robinson's *Honest to God* (1963) about God being "up there" and then "out there" and finally, "in here" is irrelevant to the believer who knows his doctrine of prayer and the Holy Spirit. Spatial location of God is immaterial. The chain of connectives is personal. It is immediate, direct and real. Would that the Bishop had looked a little harder at the biblical text and not so hard at the theologians' books:

> Whither shall I go from thy Spirit?
>   Or whither shall I flee from thy presence?
> If I ascend to heaven, thou art there!
>   If I make my bed in Sheol, thou art there!
> If I take the wings of the morning
>   and dwell in the uttermost parts of the sea,
> even there thy hand shall lead me,
>   and thy right hand shall hold me.
> If I say, "Let only darkness cover me,
>   and the light about me be night,"
> Even the darkness is not dark to thee,
>   the night is bright as the day;
>   for darkness is as light with thee.
>   PSALM 139:7–12, RSV

Wherever a Christian is, there is the Spirit! Wherever a Christian prays, the Spirit is there as the immediate connective with the mind of the Father. At the point of praying in and with the Spirit we are all mystics.

Bibliographical note:

Consult commentaries on Romans for the meaning of Romans 8:
26–27. For the meaning of *weakness* see Gustav Stählin, *"asthenēs,"*
Theological Dictionary of the New Testament. For a provoking book
on prayer I recommend Jacques Ellul, *Prayer and Modern Man*
(New York: Seabury Press, 1970).

22.

What has "the one and the many" to do with the Spirit?

The "one and the many" is an old philosophical problem. The "many" are all the particulars in the world—chairs, dogs, acts of love or justice, etc. The "one" is that which unites a certain batch of the many into one family. The "many" dogs are of the species *canis familiaris*, the "one." All the different acts of justice (the many) are supposed to participate in the one common essence which makes an act just (the one). Basically, philosophers are divided up into realists or nominalists (although there are a number of split tickets!). A realist believes that the one of the universal is more real and more important than the many which embody the universal. The nominalists believe that the universal is a grammatical tool (based on observable similarities in the world) which enables us to speak of classes (e.g., dog) in one lump without naming all the particulars. To them the particulars are more real and more important than the universals.

Oddly enough, this problem of the one and the many crops up in Christianity. We enter the kingdom one by one. We cannot baptize armies as Constantine attempted. Faith is something that is unsharable, and each believer must come his own, unique way to Christ. The church is accordingly formed one by one.

The church, however, is not like a pile of sand—individual grains—nor like a basket of wheat—individual kernels. It is a temple and a loaf; a body and one holy nation. The Spirit is that invisible linkage among believers, taking them as they come one by one into the kingdom and forming them into the one body of Christ. The many become the one by virtue of the Holy Spirit.

142

The same tension of the one and the many that pertains to philosophy also pertains to the church. The one does not absorb the many in philosophical thought but each individual has a unique and rightful existence of its own. Yet it does not stand alone. It receives its meaning as it is seen as a concrete manifestation of the one. So with the Spirit and the church! Although the Spirit unites us to the body of Christ we do not lose our unique existence as individual Christians. On the other hand, we do not stand alone but stand in the union, unity, and company of the body of Christ.

This tension is healthy. Properly understood it enables the believer to stand apart from the confessing church and proclaim its sins. The prophetic stance presumes the unique individuality of the prophet since as a member of the many he levels his criticism at the proposed one. Woe to the church which silences its prophets!

Properly understood, this tension is the preventative of undisciplined individualism. The temptation to be an Elijah and say, "Only I am left," comes out almost too clearly in Calvin! As a critic of the proposed one (the Roman Catholic church) he broke with the Roman church and went with the Reformation. But then in his *Institutes of the Christian Religion* (book 4, chapter 1, "The True Church with Which as Mother of All the Godly We must Keep Unity"), he spoke as strongly as any man has ever spoken against individualism and schism (splitting) in the history of theology. Calvin retained the tension.

Again, to repeat, this tension of the one and the many is healthy. Individual Christians who feel a special leading of the Spirit in their lives must not forget that the Spirit is the Spirit of the one. Those who see the church as the instrument through which the Spirit works must not forget the Spirit can give a gift only to an individual, not to a committee.

We are not chattering theology but talking about pragmatics. Why is it that the organized church finds it difficult or impossible to incorporate in its common life the ministry of a highly gifted, charismatic person? Why does the organized church gyrate so much to work by committees or organizations or programs or departments? Apparently a church organization is so possessed by the idea of the One that it has no flexibility to work with the charismatic individual.

In turn, the charismatic carries his share of the problem. Usually frightfully impatient with church organizations, departments, or structures, the charismatic sees the System as having clogged all the pipes through which the Spirit flows. He feels that he visualizes things with clarity whereas the average denominational secretary is in an administrative fog. Rather than try to share his charismatic powers within the one (the organized church), he finds it much easier to become an independent and enjoy the freedom of that status.

We must always be grateful for the one of the Spirit and the many of the Spirit. How horribly drab church history would be without its charismatics—St. Anthony, St. Francis, St. John of the Cross—yes, Luther (Bible student, preacher, debater, translator, organizer, educator, musician, and husband), Wesley, and many others. In turn how much work for the kingdom can only have been done by the unity of believers—missions, education, church expansion, Christian literature, hospitals, orphanages, camping. As we live in this tension of the one and the many, as individuals born of the Spirit and as the body of Christ united by the Spirit, let us not weaken it from either side, for we shall be the poorer if we do.

One further thought needs to be added. We can listen to the testimony of an individual as to how the grace of God and the Spirit of God moved mightily in his heart to convert him. As far as the human self can judge things in this world, such a person seems truly born again of the Spirit. It is much more difficult to look at the church and see it as the glorious body of Christ. C. S. Lewis in *The Screwtape Letters* (1941) tells how one of the Devil's schoolmasters coaches one of his understudy demons working here on earth. In Letter II he tells Wormwood not to let the non-Christian see a group of believers in a church as the true church which is as "terrible as an army with banners. That, I confess, is a spectacle which makes our boldest tempters tremble." Rather, Wormwood is to keep the attention of the non-Christian focused on the grubby, sweaty, ordinary character of these people. Then he will never dream who they truly are and what the church truly is.

This is because the union of believers through the Spirit is "mystical," that is, hidden. To give a testimony of the one, the total church, is almost impossible! Nevertheless, it is a reality, as witnessed in such a great book as Paul's letter to the Ephesians.

Bibliographical note:

For all the different terms used of the church, especially to express its unity, see Paul S. Minear, *Images of the Church in the New Testament* (Philadelphia: Westminster, 1960). He has summarized his materials in "Idea of the Church," *Interpreter's Dictionary of the Bible*, 1:607–617. The United Presbyterian Church in the United States of America has been one denomination that has attempted to come to terms with the one and the many in its own life. Its *Report of the United Committee on the Work of the Spirit* [face title: *The Work of the Holy Spirit*] (Philadelphia: Office of the General Assembly, 1970) is a very creative effort to come to terms with the neo-Pentecostals within their own church. For its 56 pages, it is packed with materials.

A Roman Catholic view of the one and the many may be found in Yves Congar, *The Revelation of God*, chap. 12, "The Holy Spirit and the Church" (New York: Herder and Herder, 1970). Thaddeus Horgan traces the papal encyclicals of the twentieth century, showing how the Roman Catholic Church gradually awakened to a mature doctrine of the Holy Spirit, in "An Ecumenical Theology of the Holy Spirit," The American Ecclesiastical Review, 168:145–53, September 1970.

23.

Up a tree and don't know it

Can we have a doctrine of the Holy Spirit and not have a doctrine of the Trinity? Yes, in the sense that there was a doctrine of the Spirit of God in the Old Testament. No, in the sense that the doctrine of the Trinity is the logical foundation for the doctrine of the Spirit in the New Testament. The unfolding of the doctrine of the Trinity in Patristic theology revealed how the problem of the Father and that of the Son and that of the Spirit all implicated each other. Once the nature of the Son was raised the nature of the Spirit was implicitly raised. Once the fathers pronounced the Son to be God the question was raised whether the Spirit were God. If the Son is a *persona* is not the Spirit also a *persona?* Granted that anti-Trinitarian ideas have popped up here and there in the history of the church, nevertheless it can be affirmed as a generalization that once the doctrine of the Trinity was affirmed it was not contested in the church—Roman Catholic or Protestant—until the heyday of religious liberalism. During that period the Spirit was seen as God of very God, as a Person equally with the Father and the Son, and having his unique role in the work of the Trinity.

When religious liberals denied the true deity of Christ it could not but follow that they had to deny the deity and personhood of the Holy Spirit. The historic Trinity was dissolved into some sort of functional Trinity. But the Trinity as historically understood, and the Holy Spirit as historically understood, were at an end.

Having denied the Trinity, however, theologians have not stopped talking about the Spirit. In my opinion, to attempt to talk about the Spirit while denying the doctrine of the Trinity is to be up a tree and not know it. To speak of the Spirit apart from the Trinity is to talk only of some aspect of God, and to talk of a Person possessing full deity and a special, irreplaceable role in the history of redemption.

Why do those who deny the Trinity not make a clean sweep of it? If they have reduced the Son to only the man Jesus, why not be rid of the Spirit as simply an animistic carryover from primitive Palestinian religions?

The reason that theologians who deny the Trinity still wish to speak of the Spirit can be partially explained by a look at the history of theology. One of the things that has emerged in the contest of liberalism and orthodoxy is that the foundation of all religion must be grace. It cannot be a human achievement, for if it is that, man has the right to boast. Grace excludes boasting and protects the purity of God's love. Furthermore, theologians wish to stave off a self-assertiveness in man—hubris. The Greek word *hubris* means more than pride. There is a surly element in it. Man who arrogates to himself the power to save himself is guilty of hubris.

Non-Trinitarian theologians want a theology without man's pride or goodness at the center, but rather God's grace, God's love, God's initiative at the center. In historic terms they wish to avoid the charge of Pelagianism. Pelagius was one of the great heretics of the early church who taught the essential goodness of men and thereby denied not only man's depravity but the sovereign grace of God. One of the ways of retaining the priority of divine grace and preventing men from boasting of their religious deeds is to maintain that the Holy Spirit is the source of man's spiritual life. For this reason we find that whereas theologians have unloaded the doctrine of the Trinity they still speak of the Spirit as a viable concept in Christian theology. Paul Tillich, for example, has a great deal to say of the Spirit while yet denying the historic doctrine of the Trinity.

Theologians also wish to preserve the reality of the spiritual world or the spiritual order or a spiritual dimension to life. Although theologians have denied many historic doctrines they have not become complete naturalists. They wish to see the Christian faith as grounded deeper than in the exercise of man's religious

nature, or the religious doings of many. This deeper grounding
they find in a doctrine of the Spirit. By retaining a doctrine
of the Spirit they again preserve the reality and the priority of
God in man's religious life.

The prior question remains: can a theologian have a doctrine
of the Spirit and not be up a tree? Can he deny the Trinity and
yet retain a viable doctrine of the divine Spirit? It has been my
contention that this is not possible. Granted there is no obvious
formulation of the doctrine of the Trinity in the pages of the
New Testament. On the other hand, it cannot be denied that the
New Testament is rich with Trinitarian materials. In the Gospel
of John, chapters 14–18, there is a rich interplay of relationships
of the Father to the Son, of the Son to the Spirit, and of the
Spirit to the Father. Although the Trinity is not in these passages formulated into a doctrine the references make sense only
if one presumes that doctrine. Or when we turn to the letters of
Paul and see the many statements about the Father and the Son
or the Father and the Spirit or the Spirit and the Son we find
ourselves in the same situation as with John's references. There
is an abundance of Trinitarian materials but no formulated doctrine. But the references are made clear if the doctrine is presumed. Deny the doctrine and one is left with desultory, that is,
disconnected remarks.

We should turn a deaf ear to the charge that the Trinitarian
doctrine is a piece of Greek substance philosophy intruding into
Christian theology. Ignoring Plato or Aristotle, one can, with the
materials of the New Testament, work out one's own doctrine of
the Trinity.

If the doctrine of the Trinity is denied then the doctrine of the
Spirit becomes trivial. As indicated before, it becomes a synonym
for some aspect of God such as his power or his immediacy. Even
more than this, it plunges such an expression as "the Spirit of
Christ" into obscurity. The great passages on the Second Paraclete become obscure, if not meaningless. It takes the historic
Trinitarian doctrine to make such passages meaningful.

It must also be observed that when the New Testament spoke
of the Spirit as the Spirit of Christ, the door was closed for a
retreat to the theology of the Holy Spirit of the Old Testament.
The Holy Spirit cannot be reduced to the pure presence of God

nor to a synonym for the power of God nor defined as the divine source of man's religious life. As the Spirit of Christ his fate is bound to the person of Christ. But to say that the Spirit is the Spirit of Christ is to force the doctrine of the Trinity. If we deny the Trinity we deny that the Spirit is the Spirit of Christ. If we do that, we must retreat to the Spirit as understood in the Old Testament. But that can be done only by renouncing the New Testament.

It must be repeated: to deny the doctrine of the Trinity and to continue to speak of the Holy Spirit as if he were the Spirit spoken of in the New Testament is to be up a tree and not know it.

Bibliographical note:

A sketch of what some leading recent and contemporary theologians say about the Holy Spirit may be found in J. Rodman Williams, *The Era of the Spirit* (Plainfield: Logos International, 1971). The richness of Trinitarian materials in the New Testament is discussed in Arthur W. Wainwright, *The Trinity in the New Testament* (London: SPCK, 1972). F. E. Peters, *Greek Philosophical Terms: A Historical Lexicon,* provides much useful background for possible Greek vocabulary used in theological formulations. For a defense of biblical terms lying behind the early church creeds see the exposition of these creeds in Charles A. Briggs, *Theological Symbolics* [i.e., creeds] (New York: Charles Scribner's Sons, 1914).

24.

The cure for gullibility

Ordinarily the word "gull" means a seagull. But when it is used of a human being it means a person who is easily duped, cheated, or conned. A gullible person is one who does not have aptitude in separating truth and error, fact and fiction, fable and history. It is the common assumption of people with no religious beliefs that those who hold them are gullible. The formula comes out very clear: unbelievers are sharp, clever, intelligent, shrewd, and hence not caught up with religious poppycock; believers are victims of the unsifted tradition, parental indoctrination, the slick sell, or the emotional pitch.

How does this formula sit with our doctrine of the Holy Spirit? One of the titles of the Spirit is that he is "the Spirit of truth." If Christian faith is permeated by a Spirit of truth then the charge of gullibility addressed to Christians is phony. Christians may be in error but when they are the error is one of judgment and not a disease of their Christian faith.

Naturally if people do not study Holy Scripture they do not know what is in Scripture. TRUTH is one of the big, big words of Holy Scripture. The God of Holy Scripture is a God of truth. The Word which this God speaks is the Word of truth. To believe the Word of God is to share in the truth of God. Christ is called the Truth. The gospel is the word of truth. It comes, then, as no surprise that the Spirit is called "the Spirit of truth." Our modern painful consciousness and concern for truth is anticipated for us in the same painfulness and concern for truth found in Holy Scripture.

The importance of the Spirit as being a Spirit of truth is paramount. It is the Spirit who gave us Holy Scripture. It was the

Spirit who moved the prophets to speak and then to write. The truth of the inspired Scripture implicates the Spirit who inspired it. If it is inspired Scripture it is authoritative Scripture. It is the Word of God to the church. The church must know what kind of Spirit is behind its Word.

It is the self-witness of Scripture that the Spirit which inspired it is a Spirit of truth. It certainly nowhere says that Scripture was inspired by a dishonest Spirit. Dishonesty is common among men as men are sinners but the Holy Spirit is no sinner. It is the business—*c'est son métier!*—of the Spirit to be concerned with truth. The expression "the Spirit of truth" cannot mean anything less than a person who has a passionate concern for truth.

Affirming that the Spirit who inspired Scripture is a Spirit of truth does not in itself make the Scripture true. But it does establish a footing or a beachhead, one that means in principle that the Christian is not a gullible person. The person who has a real passion for truth is not likely to be a gullible person. As in all faiths there are also gullible people in the Christian faith. However, their gullibility is a weakness in their own personality and not of the fabric of biblical revelation.

Jesus had been a Counselor to his disciples. When he left them he announced that he would send another Counselor whom he called the Spirit of Truth (John 14:17). It cannot be questioned that if any person is to be a Counselor, a Guide, and a Teacher of the disciples, he must be a person of complete veracity. If the Counselor is such a person, then those who believe in his truth are not gullible people!

A similar motif is set out in John 15:26. Our Lord again indicates that he will leave his disciples but will then send the Counselor to them. This Counselor is again called the Spirit of truth who comes from the Father. As already indicated, the entire biblical witness is that God is a God of truth. What other kind of Spirit could come from the Father but a Spirit with a passion for truth?

The theme of the Counselor is developed in greater detail in John 16:12-15. The Spirit will guide the disciples into all truth. Our concern is not with the content of that truth but that truth is the concern of the Spirit. The church needs more truth than is contained in the Gospels. The Gospels need to be supplemented by the inspired reflections of the apostles about the fullest meaning of the life of Christ. This "inspired reflection" can only truly happen if the Spirit of truth is there to truly inspire it.

In his first epistle John admonishes Christians not to be gullible (1 John 4:1–6). John says that we are not to believe every spirit but Christians are to test spirits. Spirits, however, cannot be seen or felt or interrogated in order to be tested. We can only test men and what they say and from that examination calculate the kind of spirit that inspires them. The supreme test of a spirit is whether the speaker confesses that Jesus is come in the flesh, that is, the Incarnation. If a speaker denies the Incarnation then that person is not inspired by the Spirit of God but is inspired by a spirit of error.

In another passage which shows that the Christian is not a gullible person John emphasizes that the Spirit is the witness to the truthfulness of the Christian faith (1 John 5:1–12). In this passage the word *water* means the beginning of the public ministry of Christ at his baptism; the word *blood* means the end of that ministry on the cross. We have here the external witness—the data of the life of Christ, and, the internal witness—the persuasion of the Holy Spirit. These three (water, blood, Spirit) agree (v. 8). All intend the same thing; they are all directed toward the identical result. They are all part of one seamless theological robe. Our concern is with the emphasis on the Spirit as a Spirit of truth. Here as in the Gospel of John the Spirit is a Spirit with a passion for truth—for what else can the expression "Spirit of truth" imply? Where there is this kind of Spirit there is no gullibility. No doubt tens of thousands of Christians are gullible but that is to say no more than that all amateurs in any religion are gullible. But in principle the Christian faith animated by a Spirit of truth is the least of the gullible among the religions of the world.

It is this concept of "the Spirit of truth" which is behind the Augustinian-Anselmic motto: "I believe in order to understand," or, "Faith seeks understanding," or "Faith leads, the intellect follows." The Spirit of truth demands of the Christian that once illuminated by grace he use the fullest strength of his powers and the fullest reach of his learning to explore, explain, and defend the Christian revelation.

Bibliographical note:

For a thorough commentary on the passages in John's Gospel cf.
Leon Morris, *The Gospel According to John* (Grand Rapids: Eerdmans, 1971). The Greek word for Comforter or Counselor is difficult
to translate. Cf. Johannes Behm, *"paraklētos," Theological Dictionary
of the New Testament*, 5:800–813; and Morris, pp. 662ff. A general
treatment of the Holy Spirit in John's Gospel and one of the rare
discussions in theological literature of the Holy Spirit as a Spirit of
truth may be found in George Johnston, *The Spirit-Paraclete in the
Gospel of John*, chap. 7, "Recent Studies on Paraclete and the Spirit
of Truth" (Cambridge: University of Cambridge Press, 1970). However, Johnston presses so hard on the historical and linguistic studies
he does not deal with the fuller theological implications of the materials. Note 3 on page 80 gives the fullest bibliographical references
we have seen on the history of the concept of *paraklētos*.

25.

The divine ombudsman

The Greek word *paraklētos,* translated "comforter" in the King James Version, is not an easy word to translate. It is a word with a long history and many meanings. There is perhaps a reason why John chose such a word. There are so many things the Holy Spirit will do for the Christian that only a word rich in meanings could serve as a name for the Spirit. I have chosen the Swedish word *ombudsman* to translate the Greek for the following reasons:

In the centuries before the birth of Christ the Roman government was aware of the universal tension between the ruled and the rulers, the governed and the government, Caesar and the people. If the common herd is pushed too hard it will rebel. In order to keep such pressures from building up, the Roman government established a special kind of office. A group of men were elected by the people to present their grievances to the government. These men were called *tribuni plebis* (tribunes of the people). These tribunes did not handle only one kind of complaint but all kinds of complaints.

Calvin, who was trained in both law and classics, was aware of this office in the Roman Empire for he spoke of lesser magistrates or secondary officials with a similar task. "First magistrate" refers to kings, emperors, queens, and/or other highest dignitaries. These lesser magistrates were representatives of the people appointed by the first magistrate to defend the people from all sorts of injustices. Again, Calvin's lesser magistrates were not specialized to treat one kind of injustice but all kinds.

In modern times the Scandinavians have established a similar office. The person who presents the complaint of the people to the government is the *ombudsman.* It should be noted that in prolonged usage the term has expanded in meaning to include any person who officially or unofficially helps out another person who is in some difficulty.

In my opinion this Swedish word *ombudsman* says more than any English word about the functions of the divine *paraklētos.* Both terms are a blend of the personal and judicial without being exclusively either; thus the Swedish retains the richness of the word.

At the heart of the issue is the fact that the Christian will be confronted with many kinds of problems in his Christian pilgrimage. God has not left him to his own resources but has provided the divine ombudsman. This divine ombudsman will help in all possible situations. No matter what the problem, he has the grace, the wisdom and the power for that problem.

Christ implied that he was the first ombudsman (John 14:16). If we note how Christ was an ombudsman we can understand how the Holy Spirit is one also. All the ministries of Christ to his disciples were the ministries of a paraclete, an ombudsman. Christ, in matter of fact, is even yet our ombudsman in heaven as recorded in 1 John 2:1. What person ignorant of the Greek text would have dreamed that the word translated *comforter* in John's Gospel is translated *advocate* in 1 John 2:1?

The word *paraklētos* means literally "one summoned to the side of another." So it is with the divine ombudsman. Whatever the need, the Christian has the right to summon him to his side. The same thing was also true of our Lord. He was always at the side of his disciples when they needed him and for whatever they needed him.

There is another dimension to the ombudsman not yet clarified. The function of the tribunes, lesser magistrates, and ombudsmen was to represent the people—the average person who was defenseless or without resources. They did not represent the powerful, the wealthy or the nobility. It was the very helplessness of the people that required a special kind of representation. So it is with Christians. Christians, like any other sinners, are dust and flesh so far as the resources of their own human nature are considered. Luther's famous last words that we are all beggars mean that in our spiritual poverty we all live off the grace, pity, and goodness of our heavenly Father. As poor people, weak people, and beggars, God's children need a divine ombudsman.

The non-Christian world does not know that a divine ombudsman exists (John 14:17). This is the flaw of simple theories of verification. Man cannot force all the cards onto the table. As long as he cannot do that, any theory of verification is limited. Man cannot force the Holy Spirit out into the open. Only by the word of divine revelation do we know that we have a divine ombudsman. Those ignorant of the word of revelation or who, having heard it, reject it, are not aware of the strength, courage, grace, illumination, and guidance that comes from this source.

It is also true that Christians are not aware of all that the divine ombudsman does for them. Christians only know for sure that he is there by their side from the word of revelation. In many experiences of the past we have hoped, trusted, and believed that the divine ombudsman was effectively there.

Bibliographical note:

For details on the translation of *paraklētos,* cf. bibliographical note for chapter 24. Add to that G. H. W. Lampe, ed., *A Patristic Greek Lexicon,* pp. 1018–19, and the entry entitled "Magistrate," in *Encyclopedia Britannica,* 14th ed., 14:630. For Calvin's views on "constitutional magistrates . . . to check the tyranny of kings," see his *Institutes,* IV/30, 31. Battle's translation (The Library of Christian Classics), p. 1518, fn. 54, includes an extensive note on the importance of this concept of Calvin's.

26.

In vino veritas

"*In vino veritas*," translated, reads "in wine there is truth." It refers to the well-known fact that a drunk person may babble out the truth without inhibitions—and also to the practice of getting people drunk to have them speak the truth: the first truth serum.

The Freudians state it another way. "Alcohol dissolves the superego." In Freudian psychology the superego is roughly equivalent to a person's conscience. Alcohol dissolves the inhibitions of a man's conscience so that he will say and do things he would never do when under the restraint of his conscience. "*In vino veritas*" in this light means that when the superego is rendered harmless by alcohol a person is apt to blab or blubber the truth.

Paul wrote: "And do not get drunk with wine, for that is debauchery; but be filled with the Spirit, addressing one another in psalms and hymns and spiritual songs, singing and making melody to the Lord with all your heart, always and for everything giving thanks in the name of our Lord Jesus Christ to God the Father" (Eph. 5:18–20).

There is an earthly wine and there is a heavenly wine. Just as the drinking of much earthly wine induces a different state of consciousness, so being filled with the heavenly wine induces a status of consciousness different from normal consciousness. It does not surprise us that the charge of those filled with heaven's wine should be accused of being filled with earth's wine by those who know only the wine of this earth (Acts 2:13).

If wine puts a man psychologically into a different state, the Holy Spirit puts the Christian into a different spiritual state. If earthly wine makes a man ecstatic, irrationally beside himself, then the wine of the Holy Spirit makes a Christian spiritually beside himself.

"In wine there is truth" now comes through as "in the Spirit there is truth." To keep the parallel sharp, one must say that the truest experience is in the Spirit. Or, man finds himself deepest and best through the Spirit. This statement raises the question of "the true self." Which self is the true self of a child: the child mentally and emotionally disturbed through some kind of systemic poisoning, or the child cured? Most people would say the latter. Or, which is the true child: the child who is hyperactive through brain damage or some other glandular disturbance, or the child as he is more normal through psychological medicines? Again, most people would go with the latter. So, which is the true self: the self under the domination of sin, or the self under the influence of the fullness of the Spirit? We would want to say the latter. "In the wine of the Spirit is the true self."

We may also say: "In the Spirit is the true experience." Paul describes elements of this experience. The person sings. Singing is the combination of two forms of higher, metaphorical emotional communication: poetry and music. In exalted states the human spirit leaps beyond prose to the higher ranges of communication of poesy and singing. Poetry and romantic singing have a long history in the eternal story of young love. Only such vessels can carry the load love imposes on communication. So it is with the Spirit. Only in singing can some of the fullness of the Spirit be expressed so that the self can release its burden of joy and love and others may share in the goodness of the Spirit.

We are all now passing through the dark hours of a drug culture. How long this tunnel is we do not know. One of the current expressions from the drug culture is "to be turned on." To be turned on means in some sense to be psychologically activated out of the normal state of consciousness. It is some version of ecstasy. One of the complaints of this drug generation about the church is that its services do not turn them on. No doubt the majority of church services from this standpoint are unbearably dull. But the Christian faith is not faithfully expressed in dull church services. There is the fullness of the Spirit! Here one can really be turned on! Yes, wine turned people on in Paul's day in the sense of making them ecstatic by making them tipsy. But this kind of turning on leads—in Paul's language, to *asōtia*—to dissipation! So it is with drugs. But being turned on by the Spirit leads to the most wholesome of consequences and the most blessed aftermath.

Unfortunately, there is little attention given in our usual worship services or Bible studies or prayer meetings to turning on in the Spirit. A lifeless, joyless routine service is hardly appealing to anybody—Christian or non-Christian. Furthermore, our culture which puts so much stress on the scientific, the technological, the rational, and the controlled is not at all congenial to turning on in the Spirit. Drinking of the wine of the Spirit is not an "in thing" to do. If the charismatic movement tells us anything, it tells us that people are hungering for more than the church is giving them. It tells us that there are people who yet prefer to be drunk with the Spirit in which there is no dissipation than go with the culture and be drunk with alcohol or overstimulated with drugs.

Joy is one of the most fundamental and deepest of human experiences. Without some taste of joy in life we would all sink into depression and then into nothingness and then into death. Joy keeps hope and faith alive, in turn keeping the body alive and giving the soul an appetite for life. Somewhere all real Christians have experienced the joy of the Holy Spirit. Whether they have sipped little or much of the wine of the Spirit, they have still had enough to experience its power to create joy. In these experiences Christ is most real! This is the true Christian mysticism. But here is the strength to live through all those dreary hours of life. And here is the strength to live with the dreariness of the church. We *know* what potential joy there is in Christian experience. We *know* that we can experience again and again renewals of the joy of the Holy Spirit. We can walk, then, the dreary sands for we know that around one of the turns of life there will be another oasis, another fullness of the Spirit, and with it a new transfusion of joy from that heavenly wine.

"*In vino veritas!*" Even more, "In the Spirit there is truth!" There is the truest of experiences! There is the truest expression of the self! There is participation in the truth of the Christian faith! There is the true ecstasy, the true "turning on" and the true Christian mysticism!

Bibliographical note:

We are indebted to Kierkegaard for the expression *in vino veritas*. One of the meditations in *Stages in Life's Way* (Princeton: Princeton University Press [1845]) is entitled "In vino veritas: A Recollection."

27.

A book review won't hurt

Sometimes in looking for lead one finds gold. Such was the case for me in reading Sidney M. Jourard's *The Transparent Self*.[1] This book is a series of lectures on various themes written by a counseling psychologist. One of the basic concepts Jourard works with in counseling is that of spirit-titer.

Titer is a word from chemistry which means the strength of a chemical solution. *Titration* is a special kind of procedure for finding out, for example, how strong an acid solution is. Spirit-titer would then refer to how much spirit one has. Just as an acid solution can be strong or weak, so a human personality can be strong or weak in the amount of spirit it has.

Jourard has found out experimentally that people who are well and vigorous both physically and psychologically have a lot of spirit-titer. People who are chronically ailing and psychologically fragile are people who have low spirit-titer. A doctor would like to pump some spirit-titer in his discouraged and/or depressed patients and a psychologist would like to give his neurotic counselees a shot of spirit-titer!

When a Christian sees the expression *spirit-titer* his heart skips a beat. The psychologist means by this expression only a human something such as a person's will to live, or joy of living, or vitality of the self, or vigor in facing problems. The Christian wants to read it "Spirit-titer." So we give Jourard thanks for the concept and the way he has illuminated it, but we shall go our own way with it.

---

1. New York: D. Van Nostrand Company, 1964.

165

The reason spirit-titer (and on some occasions Jourard himself uses the word *Spirit*) grabs the Christian is that he knows from reading his Scriptures that the Holy Spirit is God's immediate power. If spirit-titer is the clue to physical and mental health then the Christian has an inside track with his doctrine of the Holy Spirit, for here is a divine aid in getting us more spirit-titer—*Spirit*-titer!

The closest biblical reference to spirit-titer is the statement about Christ that the Father gave him the Spirit without measure (John 3:34). The word *metron* (measure) is used many times in the Greek New Testament. Here the expression is *ouk metron*—"not from a measure" hence, "measureless" or "without measure." All ordinary mortals can receive the Spirit only in measure (*en metron*) but the only incarnate Son of God can receive the Spirit in a measureless abundance. This is the maximum in both spirit-titer and Spirit-titer.

If one's well-being is dependent upon his spirit-titer, how does one raise the level of spirit-titer? The answer is: by inspiration. The doctor wishes to inspire his physically ill patients so that they will have a great will to get well. The psychologist wants to inspire his depressed and joyless patients so that they will have a new joy of life and love for living. But the resources of the physician and the psychologist are human, for they are concerned with spirit-titer, not Spirit-titer.

The Christian believes that he has another source for raising one's spirit-titer, that is, the divine source of Spirit-titer from which new and fresh inspiration may come. One can even diagnose Christian vitality—or lack of it—with the concept of Spirit-titer. Christians with low Spirit-titer are weak or immature or carnal Christians. Christians with lots of Spirit-titer are mature, strong, or spiritually minded Christians.

Christians with low Spirit-strength need to be inspired or "blown up" so that they have a higher Spirit-strength. Unfortunately, there is no standard formula for blowing up one's Spirit-titer. The imperative *be filled* implies that the possibility is within the Christian's grasp. "Means of grace," public and private, are other ways of increasing Spirit-titer (prayers, singing, hearing the Word preached, personal and group Bible study, the sacraments, recitation of the great things God has done as in the reports of the apostles and missionaries in the Book of Acts). In my opinion, the most important means of increasing one's Spirit-titer is by fellowship with a person or persons with lots of Spirit-titer. There is something contagious about a life that is really Spirit-filled.

Do Christians have something extra because they have Spirit-titer which non-Christians do not have? No and yes! We must first say no unless we overstate the case for Christianity. Because we do not all start our Christian life from the same place, it is impossible to have an objective measure of Spirit-titer. A Christian who starts his life from a very "disadvantaged" place may have Spirit-titer, yet in many ways be behind non-Christians who do not have Spirit-titer. Furthermore, we are still in the flesh, and justification is not glorification. A Christian in serious distress or trouble or temptation or beset by wretched problems may appear to be missing all Spirit-titer.

The answer is yes if by that we mean that a Christian has a potential the non-Christian does not have. Human spirit-titer can be reenforced by divine Spirit-titer. In theory (and we hope in practice!) Christians who are medical patients should respond faster than people without Spirit-titer. Counselors should find it a centimeter easier to lift depression in a Christian than a non-Christian if Spirit-titer is truly a factor. And Christians should respond more readily to the preached and taught Word of God because of the eagerness that is theirs as possessors of Spirit-titer.

28.

Marcion messes up the Holy Spirit

Marcion was the offbeat son of a bishop in Pontus (a territory south of the Black Sea and due east of Istanbul). He eventually came to Rome in the 140s and started a very vigorous cult of his own. He died about A.D. 160. The movement he started has been judged as the most threatening heresy the church faced in the last half of the second Christian century.

It was Marcion's contention that there were two Gods. One God was the God of the Old Testament. He was a strict and severe God whose law was the law of retaliation—lex talionis! He was also the Creator called the Demiurge by Marcion. The Greek word for demiurge means "craftsman" and was used by Plato and later by the Gnostics to refer to the one who forged the world. The God of the New Testament was a God of love and therefore radically different from the God of the Old Testament. Marcion therefore tossed out of the Christian canon the Old Testament and many of the New Testament books which didn't suit his theology. In defense of his position he wrote a book called *Antitheses* in which he painted the contrasts between the Old Testament and its God and the God of love in the New Testament.

But Marcion overlooked something about the Holy Spirit. In so doing he messed up the doctrine of the Holy Spirit. He overlooked the fact that the Old Testament contains a very rich doctrine of the Messiah and his relationship to the Holy Spirit. So rich are these materials of the Messiah and the Spirit that a study on the subject, classifying the references and showing the theology involved, was written by Robert Koch in 1950.[1]

Furthermore, it is the witness of the New Testament that it was the Spirit of Christ who inspired the prophets of the Old Testament: "The prophets who prophesied of the grace that was to be yours searched and inquired about this salvation; they inquired what person or time was indicated by the Spirit of Christ within them when predicting the sufferings of Christ and the subsequent glory" (1 Pet. 1:10–11). Very similar to this is a verse in the Book of Revelation: "For the testimony of Jesus [i.e., that which witnesses to who he is] is the spirit of prophecy" (19:10b). In harmony with this is Philip's reply to the Ethiopian eunuch who asked him whom Isaiah 53 was written about. Philip said it was written about Jesus.

If the Holy Spirit who produced the Old Testament is the Spirit of Christ—and, as Koch's book shows, the Spirit is already in the Old Testament as the Spirit of the Messiah—how then can Marcion lop off the Old Testament from the Christian canon without messing up the canon? If the burden of prophecy is Jesus Christ the Messiah, how can one pit the God of the Old Testament against the God of the New Testament? When Marcion does this he messes up the doctrine of the Spirit.

Marcion did snip off New Testament books too, but not the Gospel of Luke. In Luke's Gospel the risen Lord opens the minds of his disciples so that they can see him in "the law of Moses and the prophets and the psalms" (i.e., the whole Old Testament Canon; Luke 24:44–47). Even Marcion's own New Testament canon is against him!

Marcionism stands in theology for any effort either to cut off the Old Testament canon or so to interpret it that it really ceases to be a Christian book in that its Messianic witness is muted. We have a literal case of Marcionism in the Nazi German Christian Church. Because the Old Testament was written by Jews, it was repudiated and ancient Teutonic mythology put in its place. All Old Testament scholars who reject the Messianic content of the Old Testament because they reject the supernatural revelation implicit in such an understanding of the Old Testament are really Marcionites. They accuse those who do find

---

1. *Geist und Messias* (Vienna: Verlag Herder, 1950).

Christ in the Old Testament of reading Christ back into the Old Testament.

The case of Bultmann, the famous German New Testament scholar and theologian, is interesting. He can hardly cut off the Old Testament and still be in the good graces of his fellow scholars. He does, however, deny that it has any Christological predictions. The function of the Old Testament, in his view, is to show the existential failure of man under the law.

Granted, there has been the temptation to see too much of Christ in the Old Testament. Hengstenberg in the nineteenth century and Wilhelm Vischer in the twentieth have been judged guilty of this fault. Some of Barth's Christological interpretations of the Old Testament are considered pure allegorisms. Fundamentalists usually let their typology run riot in allegorical interpretation.

But the abuse of the Christological element in the Old Testament is not sufficient excuse for refutation of the Christological element. If we are going to be true to the Messiah-Spirit teaching of the Old Testament and the New Testament claim that the Spirit of prophecy is the Spirit of Christ then we cannot hold to any kind of Marcionism. If we do, we mess up the doctrine of the Spirit just as Marcion did.

Bibliographical note:

In their effort to avoid the older scheme of seeing obvious Christological passages in the Old Testament as predicting obvious Christological passages in the New Testament, Old Testament scholars have been very busy trying to find new ways of relating the Old to the New Testament. Some of these tend to lean very much in the direction of Marcion, namely, that the Old Testament in no real sense is a Christological document. Cf. the opinions in Claus Westermann, *Essays on Old Testament Interpretation* (London: SCM Press, 1960).

29.

The ugly ditch of history

The German dramatist Lessing (1729–1781) spoke of "the ugly ditch" of history. By this expression he meant that events of the past were forever gone and could never be retrieved. Consequently no event of the past could have meaning for the present except in the sense that we live in consequence of these events. Because the American general Washington defeated the British troops with his colonial armies we in this country today are all citizens of the United States of America. But no living American can have a personal or "existential" relationship with Washington. The ugly ditch of history separates us.

If Lessing is right then Christianity as it has been understood is impossible. Since the basis of the biblical revelation is history, *and* if Lessing is right, the ugly ditch of history separates us from that biblical history so that it can have no real meaning for us. Furthermore, the gospel is centered in the historical career of Jesus Christ. If the ugly ditch of history separates us from Christ, then the death and resurrection of Christ can have no meaning for us.

Luther thought of this problem long before Lessing, and Kierkegaard, who tried to answer Lessing with his unique understanding of the Incarnation. Luther found his answer in the doctrine of the Holy Spirit as the Spirit of Christ. The gospel rests on the possibility of Jesus Christ's being a living reality to men of every generation. How does Jesus Christ leap the ugly ditch of history? According to Luther, it is the Holy Spirit who takes the Jesus of the gospels, the Jesus of history, the Jesus of the Gospel, and makes him a living reality to faith.

Luther faced another problem upon which Lessing and Kierkegaard did not focus. Christ ascended and is in heaven. Here is
an ugly spatial ditch. Again the premise of the gospel is that
Christ is present in the act of faith; and Christ indwells the
believer. How does the exalted Christ at the right hand of God
close the perpendicular ditch between himself and the man of
faith? Again Luther appealed to the theology of the Holy Spirit.
It is the Holy Spirit who makes the ascended and exalted Christ
a living reality to the man of faith.

174

Bibliographical note:

Cf. George S. Hendry, *The Holy Spirit in Christian Theology*, chap. 4, "The Holy Spirit and the Word."

30.

We close with a poem

Robert Herrick (1591–1674) belonged to the great age of English literature. His fame rests primarily on his poems of English town and country life. Although he was a minister, there was nothing remarkable about Herrick from that perspective except the story that once, when exasperated with the inattention of his congregation to his sermon, he wrathfully threw his sermon manuscript at it. He was a humorist, a quality that creeps out in the poem we shall cite below.

There are few hymns to the Holy Spirit and scarcely a good one. Poems about the Holy Spirit are even rarer. In my opinion none matches Robert Herrick's and I feel there is no better way of ending this rap session about the Holy Spirit than to follow good sermonic wisdom and quote:

HIS LITANY TO THE HOLY SPIRIT

In the hour of my distress,
When temptations me oppress,
And when I my sins confess,
    Sweet Spirit, comfort me!

When I lie within my bed,
Sick in heart and sick in head,
And with doubts discomforted,
    Sweet Spirit, comfort me!

When the house doth sigh and weep,
And the world is drowned in sleep,
Yet mine eyes the watch do keep,
    Sweet Spirit, comfort me!

When the artless doctor sees
No one hope, but of his fees,
And his skill runs on the lees,
  Sweet Spirit, comfort me!

When his potion and his pill,
Has, or none, or little skill,
Meet for nothing but to kill,
  Sweet Spirit, comfort me!

When the passing-bell doth toll,
And the furies in a shoal
Come to fright a parting soul,
  Sweet Spirit, comfort me!

When the tapers now burn blue,
And the comforters are few,
And that number more than true,
  Sweet Spirit, comfort me!

When the priest his last hath prayed,
And I nod to what is said,
'Cause my speech is now decayed,
  Sweet Spirit, comfort me!

When, God knows, I'm tossed about,
Either with despair or doubt,
Yet, before the glass is out,
  Sweet Spirit, comfort me!

When the tempter me pursu'th
With the sins of all my youth,
And half damns me with untruth,
  Sweet Spirit, comfort me!

When the flames and hellish cries
Fright mine ears and fright mine eyes,
And all terrors me surprise,
  Sweet Spirit, comfort me!

When the Judgment is revealed,
And that opened which was sealed,
When to thee I have appealed,
  Sweet Spirit, comfort me!